To Sam

With best wishes
and sincere
appreciation for
you advice, counsel,
criticism and mentoring!

Seth G. Goldsmith
Nov 21, 1977
Amherst

AMBULATORY CARE

Seth B. Goldsmith, Sc. D.

ASPEN SYSTEMS CORPORATION
GERMANTOWN, MARYLAND
1977

Library of Congress Cataloging in Publication Data

Goldsmith, Seth B.
Ambulatory care

Bibliography: p. 125
Includes index

1. Hospitals—Outpatient services. 2. Hospitals—United States—
Outpatient services. 3. Group medical practice. 4. Group medical
practices—United States.
I. Title. [DNLM: 1. Ambulatory care. WX205 G623a]
RA974.G64   362.1'2   77-10315
ISBN 0-912862-46-7

Library of Congress Catalog Card Number: 77-10315
ISBN:0-91862-46-7

Printed in the United States of America.
1 2 3 4 5

To

Jonas and Benjamin

Table of Contents

Preface

On July 25, 1977, the *New York Times* featured a story about the conflict at the Hunterdon Medical Center between the hospital-based specialist medical staff and the hospital's board and administration over the issue of the future of nonhospital-based private specialty practice. The immediate problem which resulted in an opthalmologist's resignation and subsequent reappointment to the staff with admitting privileges (although she is not now hospital based) is seemingly resolved. However, still to be decided are the key issues of specialist/family practitioner relationships and the future role of the hospital in Hunterdon County, which are identified and discussed in Chapter 8.

The newspaper report illustrates both the dynamic nature of the case study approach and the obvious limitation of timeliness with this method. Indeed, subsequent to the preparation of many of these cases, satellite operations have been opened, key staff have died or resigned, new personnel have been recruited, reorganizations have taken place and myriad other changes have occurred. Despite these changes, however, the essential points illustrated by the cases presented remain relevant.

It should be noted that this book is the product not only of extensive review and reading in ambulatory care but also of over fifty field visits undertaken over a period of several years. The cases selected and developed attempt to synthesize major analytical points and principles and allow further review and discussion for the experienced health and hospital administrator as well as the student. It is the hope of the author that this expectation is attained.

Seth B. Goldsmith
September 1977

Acknowledgments

A work such as this is the result of a long and often complicated process that involved input from literally hundreds of persons —administrators, physicians, researchers, trustees, and consumers. To all of these people, who are really too numerous to list, I wish to express my thanks for their advice, insights, and support.

Special thanks are due to my friend and colleague, Bill Ferretti, for his chapter; Ron Day, my former research associate, for his bibliographic work and his continual assistance; Floyd Taylor and Joe Davis for their work with the manuscript; and, of course, my many colleagues at Columbia for their valuable assistance and criticism.

Chapter 1

Ambulatory Care: An Introduction

Most people obtain most of their medical care on an ambulatory basis, and most of that care is delivered in doctors' offices. However, there is a definite trend toward the institutionalization of ambulatory care; specifically, hospitals, group practices, medical schools, and private entrepreneurs are increasingly getting into the business of ambulatory care.

This book is about the administration and organization of institutionally based ambulatory care. The cases describe real organizations; in some instances several organizations have been synthesized and the name or location changed for total candidness in the case presentation. Some of these organizations were originally studied as part of a project undertaken at the Columbia University Center for Community Health Systems and School of Public Health and funded by the Robert Wood Johnson Foundation, while others were researched in the course of activities directly related to the preparation of this book.

The format is unusual in the health field since the cases are presented with both a general introduction and subsequent commentary. The first chapter offers an overview of ambulatory care, exploring definitional problems and presenting a range of perspectives. Part I then focuses on group practice, with a basic theory of group practice and the reality of three actual groups. Part II gives a critical assessment of multi-specialty ambulatory care in three case studies. Part III considers hospital-based primary care and presents two cases. A final chapter reviews some earlier points and offers concluding remarks.

AMBULATORY CARE: TOWARD A DEFINITION

The term "ambulatory care" was comprehensively defined by F. A. Wilson and D. Neuhauser in *Health Services in the United States* as:

> Care rendered to patients who come to physicians' offices, outpatient departments, and other health centers. However, it often includes by extension other hospital related, non-patient components of care such as emergency and home care services.[1]

A common misconception about ambulatory care is that the patient is "walking." This often is not the case. As M.M. Stewart and C.H. Goodrich have noted,[2] individuals availing themselves of ambulatory care services may arrive in wheelchairs and stretchers. Indeed, the general and important theme in the Wilson-Neuhauser definition is not that the patients are walking, but rather that they are capable of being moved some distance, normally from a domicile other than a hospital to another facility.

If there is an "official" definition of ambulatory care it is probably the one offered by J.B. Tenney, K.L. White, and J.W. Williamson, which is incorporated into the *National Ambulatory Medical Care Survey:* "It (ambulatory care) is defined as health services rendered individuals under their own cognizance, at a time when they are not in a hospital or other health care institution."[3]

Basically then, ambulatory care can be thought of algebraically as equal to 1-X, where 1 represents all personal health services, while X stands for all those services provided to inpatients of institutions such as hospitals and nursing homes.

Confounding the thinking on the issues of ambulatory care are a second grouping of terms: primary, secondary, and tertiary care. Primary care is not necessarily synonymous with ambulatory care; indeed, many primary care practitioners admit and care for a large number of inpatients in thousands of community hospitals. Primary care refers to ambulatory and inpatient care that tends to be general medical care in nature and is likely to be first contact care. While most often provided by what is thought of as a primary care practitioner, such as an internist, pediatrician or the family practitioner, there are instances of urologists, neurosurgeons, and psychiatrists functioning as primary care practitioners for individuals and families.

Perhaps what most differentiates primary care from secondary or tertiary care is the idea of referral. Under a highly structured system, such as the British National Health Service, the patient is obliged to see a general practitioner before seeing another level of care such as a dermatologist. In such a system the different levels of care are clear. Under a less structured system, such as our own, patients can and do refer themselves to the varying levels of care. However, as is evident from the dermatology illustration, level of care is not synonymous with ambulatory/nonambulatory status. Indeed, the distinction will continue to be further clouded with such developments as hospital-based ambulatory surgical units.

FACTORS PRECIPITATING CHANGES IN AMBULATORY CARE

A variety of social, economic, and political forces have converged in most of the organizations studied to produce ambulatory care changes.

The single most significant social factor is one of philosophical approach, that is, a perceived responsibility about the delivery of medical care. Many institutions have been clearly committed to excellence, but over time the definition of excellence has changed. Blueprints for tertiary or secondary care facilities and programs require reevaluation, and community needs dictate that change is necessary.

Other social factors that may be affecting the movement toward change include the socialization that physicians are now receiving as the result of their medical-school experience. For example, one young physician who is a member of a group practice stated during an interview:

> I spent my entire professional training—internship, residency, and fellowship—in a medical school setting. I have always been able to call upon multi-specialty capabilities and have always had a chance to interact with people in my own profession. Essentially, then, I have never functioned in an isolated setting—I guess I enjoy working with people. So, really, I guess I was just group-oriented on the basis of my personality, background, and past experience . . . as far as going into solo practice or going into a group, obviously one of the big features of going into a group was having the setup available to handle the business aspects of medicine, which I really don't like to get all that involved in. I'm

a lot more comfortable if I don't have to do all that stuff. . . . It
was a lot more threatening to me (business) than it is now,
because I've learned a little bit about business in medicine since.

Suggested in the thoughts of this physician are several ideas.
First, there is the general concept that it is organizationally easier to
practice in a group setting than a non-group setting. This may
simply be because this individual was trained in a group setting and
does not know those aspects of solo practice that have obviously made
it attractive to physicians for the past several decades. Second, he
implied that there are certain legal risks in practicing alone. Specifically, physicians practicing without the benefit of consultative services and high quality ancillary services are in some senses putting
themselves at a higher risk for not practicing within a community's
expected standard, which tends to be the standard practiced at
medical schools. Finally, there is the implied physical risk of
practicing alone, a risk related to life style and nonmedical interests.
Interviews indicate that younger doctors, while totally committed
professionally to the practice of medicine, have a wide range of
interests outside of medicine. They want organizational forms which
allow them to pursue the practice of excellent medicine while simultaneously developing themselves in a range of other activities.

The economic and political factors precipitating change are usually
not as clearly delineated or articulated as such social factors. For
example, a major factor moving institutions into ambulatory care
business is that of declining in-patient occupancy. The hope and
expectation is that if a certain group of patients can be "catch-
mentized," then a referral pattern can be established whereby those
individuals needing hospitalization or secondary or tertiary care
services will logically find their way to the institution responsible for
primary care services. Of course this is defensive administrative
medicine. Hospital administrators and others are recognizing the
increasingly competitive nature of medical care in a community.
They are also realizing that unless they take steps to insure the
viability of their institution, the declining occupancy rate may
eventually bring them to the situation of 17 New York City hospitals
in the fall of 1974—bankrupt.

This reality becomes even more important as community hospitals
throughout America acquire more sophisticated diagnostic and
treatment facilities and better-trained physicians. Indeed, as physicians become more closely aligned with one institution, they also
become responsible for that hospital's occupancy. In order to practice

secondary and tertiary care medicine, these physicians need some mechanism to feed in the primary care patients. It is highly unlikely that primary care physicians in a community are going to refer patients to a hospital which has essentially closed them out. Thus, a hospital must develop its own total health care system in order to survive.

PROBLEMS OF CHANGE

Any change, particularly in a medical institution, brings a number of significant conceptual and pragmatic problems. Among the most important conceptual problems are those related to the attitudes of physicians. For example, in one organization study, a certain amount of tension was found between those young physicians who tend to be somewhat more community medicine oriented and the older physicians whose tradition is that of fee-for-service specialty practice. Even in instances where there is agreement that a given problem exists, there is often disagreement over the solution. Some people may think that a poorly functioning outpatient department should be closed down, while others think that building it up is the answer. It is important to note, though, that over time, once the change becomes implemented and takes root, there tends to be support for the new program throughout the organization. Other conceptual problems involve the implications of change. For example, what does it really mean to be in a medical office building in group practice?

A final conceptual problem worth noting is the ancient shibboleth of the corporate practice medicine. In the past, this was an issue that generated considerable interest and controversy. However, it now appears to have died a gentle and natural death. The Judas of the past, such as the Oschner Clinic group in New Orleans, is now the backbone of organized medicine. Indeed, the county medical society in Hunterdon County is made up almost exclusively of physicians who are primary-care practitioners in the county and specialists at the Hunterdon Medical Center, while the society's president is now, by tradition, the medical director of the Hunterdon Medical Center.[4]

Other problems of change include the governance of the new units, the decisions that must be made about the services to be offered, the financing of services, and delineation of the patient population to be served by the institution.

Governance is rather critical when the new or separate structure is being developed. For example, in some cases one sees ambulatory care made ultimately responsible to the hospital's board of trustees, but a separate advisory board being developed to function as a policy-planning and sometimes governing board for that program. In other instances, separate organizations are made essentially responsible for primary care, with an overseer type of medical staff committee acting as a general governing board for the primary care services. However, where the responsibility is diffused throughout the organization, governance of the ambulatory care services is similarly diffused. Thus, in some institutions, the *general* responsibility for primary care is with the administration of the total organization, but the *specific* responsibility for services is at a much lower and direct service organizational level, such as the department of emergency care.

The basic point that emerges is that varying levels of consciousness exist about ambulatory care. The greater the level of consciousness, the more likely that there is some formal governing structure, as well as direct planning and clear authority and responsiblity for the services.

What professional services should be offered and how they should be offered is another important question that must be faced by all organizations developing ambulatory care programs. Again, the level of how they face these questions differs from organization to organization.

Thus, when a group starts anew, it has to make a conscious decision about the services to be offered, what backup services should be immediately available, and what should be contracted for. On the other hand, when programs are developed as "add ons" to other programs, they must also develop in some concert with already existing programs. In the clearest situations, decisions about the services to be offered in primary care would evolve from good information on the population's health needs. In the cases under review, such information was either not available or in the process of being developed.

FINANCING

Fiscal problems are, without question, an area of major concern to all parties involved with organizing and delivering ambulatory care services. Some of the fiscal headaches when the program is hospital-related are concerned with reimbursement rates and cost allocation. Another problem of equal importance is that of capital financing. Where is the hospital going to get funds for additional buildings? Along with this is the requirement to obtain a certificate of need approval, as well as a favorable rendering in a financial and/or marketing feasibility study when new construction or significant renovation is required. On the other hand, some of these problems can be minimized when the primary care program is incorporated with other ongoing programs, such as emergency services or an outpatient department. This may eliminate the need for significant physical renovation.

Interrelated with the financial aspects of primary care are the points mentioned earlier. The occupancy rates for certain areas, such as medicine and surgery, as well as utilization of ancillary services, are the life line of the institution. This means that the hospital must gradually achieve the appropriate number of beds—which may mean converting some to other uses, such as long-term or ambulatory care—and it must have programs to attract both patients and physicians. The physical facility is of great importance in any ambulatory care program. Present locations usually offer the major conceptual and practical constraints on development. This situation is illustrated by myriad institutions who see themselves as "trapped" in a downtown location with a patient population moving to the suburbs. One possible and popular answer is the providing off-site locations. Building the facility is usually not difficult; but problems do arise in deciding the location and the staffing. For example, how do you get physicians to practice in satellite clinics? Should the physicians practicing in the satellites be the same ones who practice in the hospital's primary care center?

Within present physical facilities, there is usually a problem of too little space. Appointment systems and flexibility of physical design often seem to go a long way toward maximally utilizing a crowded area. Unfortunately, the least aesthetically pleasing facilities, such as some prefabricated office buildings, often tend to be the most functional in the long run, while the most interesting and imaginative facilities are sometimes limited functionally because of a lack of flexibility and a physical inability to meet patient demands for growth.

PATIENT POPULATION

A major problem of change is the question who will be served by the new program. Often it is thought that the totally disenfranchised patient should be the beneficiary of the new ambulatory care program. However, as has been repeatedly demonstrated, a program's viability may depend on mixing patients from all socioeconomic classes. Further, when one offers a first-class primary care service, it is not easy to "turn off patients." Certain patient populations will walk in and seek acute care, perhaps care for an entire episode, but may not come back. The question is, how does an institution go about defining and "capturing" a population?

This question has most clearly been addressed by the Hunterdon Medical Center, which has defined its catchment area as the county population. Being the only hospital provider of health services in the county, a not unusual situation, makes this definition of patient population somewhat easier. Nevertheless, in situations where a catchment area is fairly well defined, one does see a less assertive stance than Hunterdon's toward providing health care for the population.

In sum, there are numerous problems associated with change from being a traditional inpatient or secondary and tertiary care provider of services, but all of these problems might come under the rubric of developing clear objectives for health care delivery programs. In instances where clear objectives for primary care are defined, there appears to be a flow of clear organizational authority and responsibility for care and a subsequent clear delineation of services to be offered to populations.

PROGRAM OUTCOMES

The *caveat* in this area is that little evaluation has yet taken place. Nevertheless, we do find in some limited situations a number of fairly positive outcomes from developing ambulatory care programs. First, a grouping of physicians in some instances offers an opportunity for continual peer consultation, peer review, and the likelihood of higher care quality for patients. The sharing of information, services, and plans represents a tremendous potential in terms of the quality and quantity of services available for a population. In the most highly organized programs, this potential probably comes closest to being realized. However, even in those instances where a program is fairly diffuse, the parent structure within which an ambulatory care program finds itself often offers some of the basic advantages of group practice.

A second program outcome relates to the basic status of ambulatory care within the organization of a total health system. Perhaps the clearest example is the family practice units associated with the Hunterdon Medical Center, in which there is no question that family practice is accorded first-class status. Physicians are practicing in these units because they want to; they are providing primary and family-centered care as a bona fide *raison d'etre*, and it is probable that high physician and patient satisfaction result from this. Indeed, in a situation such as Hunterdon County, where the Hunterdon Medical Center has developed an environment clearly conducive to the practice of primary care, physicians graduated from the family practice residency have over time settled in that community. This suggests that when an institution can provide an organized and hospitable environment for practicing primary and ambulatory care, whether it be within the hospital's total organizational framework or as a hospital-sponsored extramural activity, such as at Hunterdon, physicians will find the arrangement satisfying, stable, and challenging enough to continue the program.

Patient satisfaction with the programs is another important outcome. Based on the patient interviews carried out during these case studies, it was found that patients were satisfied, hoped to continue their relationship with primary-care providers, and would recommend the programs to friends and family. Indeed, one might go so far as to ask what could not be satisfying, for patients are treated in all these instances in a warm and cordial way, their relationship with the physician is confidential, and the services are convenient, available, and obviously patient-centered.

PROGNOSTICATIONS

Considering the future, three assumptions might be made. First, some type of national health insurance will initially shift the burden of payment, but will eventually result in a drastic reorganization of the health system. Second, physicians are looking for organizational entities most congenial to the way they have been trained to practice medicine; thus, the interest in medical care foundations, health maintenance organizations, and group practices. Third, hospitals are trying to define the population to which they will be most responsible. In a sense, hospitals are seeking to become the "Health Care Corporations" discussed by the Perloff report several years ago.[5]

These three developments suggest that hospitals no longer can simply take a hands-off approach to ambulatory care—that is, they cannot allow it to be practiced by community physicians who have no relationship to the institution. Indeed, hospitals will have to be concerned with who is practicing ambulatory care and what is happening to patients who cannot receive ambulatory care from those offering the services.

CONCLUSION

All of the organizations reviewed in this book are doing something different in ambulatory care; that is, something different from what they have been doing and from what may be done by other organizations. Each of the programs developed because of the individual problems, constraints and needs of the hospitals in the community. Although no program is clearly replicable in total, there are aspects and process factors that would no doubt be of value to any organization thinking about its future in primary care.

NOTES

1. F.A. Wilson and D. Neuhauser, *Health Services in the United States* (Cambridge: Ballinger Publishing Co., 1974), p. 183.

2. M.M. Stewart and C.H. Goodrich, "Special Problems of Primary Care in Large Urban Hospitals," *Community Hospitals and the Challenge of Primary Care* (New York: Center for Community Health Systems, Columbia University, 1975), p. 107.

3. J.B. Tenney, K.L. White, and J.W. Williamson, *National Ambulatory Medical Care Survey: Background and Methodology in National Center for Health Statistics* (Washington, D.C.: Government Printing Office, April 1974), p. 1.

4. For a good general background about the Hunterdon Medical Center, readers are advised to review H.B. Curry et al., *Twenty Years of Community Medicine* (Frenchtown, N.J.: Columbia Publishing Co., 1974).

5. American Hospital Association, "Report of Special Committee on the Provision of Health Services" (Chicago: American Hospital Association, 1970).

Part I
Group Practice

Chapter 2

Group Practice: Toward a Pragmatic Theory

INTRODUCTION

Group practice is a central idea in much of what is occurring in ambulatory care. The literature of group practice tends to fall into several categories: definitions and analyses of trends, reviews of particular problems or issues faced by fee-for-service and/or prepaid practices, or polemics on the cost and benefits of group practices for society, consumers, or doctors.

Rather than attempt to provide a status report on group practice, I will offer a hierarchial theory that seems to explain much about the present organization and development of group practices.

THE BASIC THEORY

The essence of group practice is sharing. Sharing is defined in a variety of ways, ranging from experiencing something with others to giving others part of what is earned by oneself. Some sharing is clearly nonthreatening; for example, Harry Truman allegedly said that sharing one's surplus is not sharing at all. Other sharing, however, represents some degree of personal or professional sacrifice.

The basic mechanical theory of group practice is that there are three levels of sharing, each level is clear and distinct, each level has a variety of sublevels, and each level must be negotiated before the next level can be reached. Further, each level offers real and conceptual costs and benefits to consumers and practitioners.

Level I is the administrative level and the most basic level for any group practice. In a sense it is an organizational analogue of Dr. Abraham Maslow's Survival and Security levels. Level II is the professional level, most easily characterized by the sharing of professionally relevant information. The final level is the synthesis of the group into something more than the aggregation of people—in popular terms, the three musketeers approach, "one for all and all for one."

Level I: Administrative

There is no point in three physicians going into a group practice if they all plan to maintain separate offices in separate buildings, hire separate nurses and receptionists, have separate telephones, supplies, and so forth.

Group practices presuppose some sharing and some economies related to that sharing. At the most basic sublevel, this might include the sharing of a physical facility and the utilities of that plant, such as gas, electric and telephone service. One step up would take us to the sharing of those physical facilities that are more physically and spiritually related to a doctor, such as a waiting room. The sharing of administrative services, such a receptionist, secretary or billing clerk, might be somewhere in the middle of this level. Near the top of this level is the sharing of the nonphysician health professionals who work in these types of settings, such as nurses and laboratory technicians.

It is not sharing to hire a nurse who works exclusively with one physician and can be dismissed by that physician. It is sharing when part of the nurse's work week is spent with other physicians and the nurse's tenure of appointment is not solely at the discretion of a single doctor. At the top of the administrative level is the conceptual surrender by a group of physicians of their adminstrative authority and responsibility to a disinterested third party, namely an administrator. Hiring an administrator, it is suggested, is also the attainment of the top rung on the administrative level. It means that the group has implicitly or explicitly agreed to share a range of administrative functions in an impersonal and non-self-serving basis.

The successful negotiation of this level by a group of physicians is potentially rewarded by an easing of the administrative and overhead burden and a flexibility not otherwise possible. Thus, three physicians sharing a waiting room, receptionist, clerk/secretary and five nurses might be more efficient than each having a separate waiting room and staff. A sick nurse does not bog down the operation in such a setup as one would in the "separate but equal" situation. The cost to physicians is an obvious loss of autonomy—that is, they are longer able to have sole charge of directing their nonprofessional activities.

The patient's experience at this level is probably at most a subtle sense of depersonalization and a (potentially) slightly smaller bill. For example, if you were used to seeing one doctor, receptionist, and nurse, and then you were shifted into a waiting room shared by another doctor's patients, etc., you might feel that the personal touch was somewhat lost. On the other hand, since the practice would be saving money by not duplicating personnel and facilities, it is possible that some percent would be reflected in the cost of medical care.

To society, such an arrangement can have positive economic impact and a potential for offering better, more available, and more accessible medical care than an individual entrepreneurial style of operating.

Level II: Professional

The professional level of sharing is a second major rung up on the hierarchy ladder and relates to activities more clearly within the physician's professional jurisdiction. These are also not very threatening. Two sublevels might be defined. The lowest is illustrated by an activity such as using a common medical record for all the patients in the practice. A more threatening and higher level of commitment to sharing occurs when group members agree to share one another's patients. Such sharing can result from cross-coverage arrangements or when patients accept several doctors as their physicians.

The implications of a group practice moving to this level of sharing are profound. To the doctor it means giving up some autonomy vis-a-vis a patient: "the patient can be handled by others" ... "I'm now one of three gods." Perhaps of greater significance is the potential of such a sharing. It could mean the beginning of an informal peer review mechanism with concomitant rewards and sanctions, such as a professionally higher quality practice or the freezing out of physicians who are practicing in a marginal way.

For the patient, a certain depersonalization and apparent, as well as sometimes relative, fragmentation can occur. This happens, for example, when the patient begins to be a one-inch thick medical record and not a person. On the other hand, if some type of quality and utilization review are taking place as a result of this sharing, the patient stands to gain in an important technical way.

The societal costs and benefits must also be classified in a theo-
retical way. With professional sharing, the benefits accruing to an
individual eventually accrue to a society. Lawyers might like to point
out that sharing sometimes leads to collusion and then destructive
monopolistic practices. Physicians must query, "Is that what we
want?"

Level III: Personal

The highest level is the personal level of sharing, according to this
theory. Four elements of personal sharing are suggested: philosophy,
professional review, money, and the future.

The first, philosophy, may seem a bit ethereal, but it is actually
quite significant. From an operational perspective, it means that the
group's physicians have sat down together and thought about,
articulated, and in some ways resolved their reasons for being in a
group and how they will relate to one another. It should be an honest
appraisal and acceptance of the strengths, weaknesses, and implications of a relationship. Such a philosophic sharing also suggests that
a group that has made this peace within itself can be more helpful
and responsive to the physicians it interviews for membership in the
group.

The professional review sharing is highly sensitive and represents
an extremely important stage of personal maturation. It means that
physicians can and do review one another with the expectation that
these reviews will be helpful in improving an individual's practice
and that this review is professional and not personal. A family
analogy might bring this into focus: It essentially is a step whereby
everyone has agreed to live together "until death do us part," but
everyone has also agreed to help each other reach their maximum
potential. The professional review can take many forms—periodic
conferences, chart reviews, or colleague observations. The method,
however, is far less important than the principle that individual
physicians have agreed to reveal themselves to their peers, the peers
have agreed to an honest appraisal, the reviewee has agreed to take
the advice and counsel to heart, and all have agreed to continue to
work together.

The third personal sharing element, money, is in some ways the
most interesting because it is so often a surrogate for the levels and
sublevels of the entire theory. At this highest level, everyone would
know everyone else's "business," that is, how much was billed and

how much paid out to the doctor. Based on observations of a number of group practices, it appears that this theoretically occurs quite often—I say theoretically, because there are very subtle ways for this information to be theoretically available, but practically unavailable. For example, in one large midwestern group practice, all the information on billings and income was kept in the group manager's secretary's office and any partner could review the data, but not remove the file from the office. Effectively, anyone who wished to review his seventy partners' data was considered nosey, and it would probably take two weeks to cull through the data and put it into any meaningful form. A contrasting example might be a group that provided each doctor with a periodic income and disbursement report of all the physicians.

Clearly, the most ambiguous element of this personal level is the future. The idea here is that the sharing of a common vision of the future is an important commitment within a group. Whether the group agrees that it should work toward a tripling in size over the next decade or that it should never accept any new patients or partners is irrelevant. What is important is that a common investment goal is identified and all group members are working toward that goal. Basically, then, the goal of the individual professional is in large measure congruent with the goal of the larger group.

The implications of this level to the doctors are critical. It gives them a commitment and reorganizational roots that potentially allow them to grow professionally and mature with a minimum of friction. To the patient it offers an opportunity for continuity of higher quality care. And to the overall health system, it represents a potentially valuable and healthy element.

Real dangers, however, also exist. Such close sharing also represents an opportunity for collusion, monopoly, and poor quality, high-priced care. Obviously, the specific direction of a group depends on a host of variables that will probably be most influenced by the value system of the group's formal and informal leaders.

THE GROUP PRACTICE CASES

The following three cases illustrate the reality of group practices. The first two groups are multispecialty freestanding, that is, not hospital based or affiliated, and the third is a small family-practice group. In the Colorado Springs case, we see a group facing many serious problems that has moved in the direction of "profes-sionalizing" its administration. It has certainly gone through the administrative and professional levels on the hierarchy and is now maturing within the personal level. The second group appears to be somewhat caught on the lower rungs of the professional level and provides an interesting contrast to the Colorado Springs case. In the Sunset case, we observe and analyze the coming together of a small group.

REFERENCES

As noted, this chapter offers a theory of group practice and does not pretend to be a review of the literature or even an operations manual for group practices. However, for the reader who wishes to learn more about group practice, the following basic references are offered.

Center for Research in Ambulatory Health Care Administration, Medical Group Management Association. *The Organization and Development of a Medical Group Practice.* Cambridge: Ballinger, 1976.

Pollack, Jerome. *The Grouping of Medical Practice in Community Hospitals and Primary Care.* Boston: Ballinger, 1976.

An excellent review article on the historical development of group practices.

Rorem, Rufus. *Private Group Clinics.* Chicago: University of Chicago Press, 1931; reprinted 1971 by the Milbank Memorial Fund, New York.

A fascinating research report originally undertaken by the Committee on the Costs of Medical Care. An historical must.

Two organizations with libraries of materials on group practice are:

American Group Practice Association
Box 949, 20 S. Quaker Lane
Alexandria, Virginia 22313
703-751-1000

Medical Group Management Association
4101 E. Louisiana Avenue
Denver, Colorado 80222
303-753-1111

Chapter 3

Colorado Springs Medical Center

Since the spring of 1972, the 32-man Colorado Springs Medical Center (CSMC) entered into what might be described as the third major phase in its evolution—planned growth and development. The first evolutionary phase began in December, 1946, when eight physicians, supported by five nonprofessionals, opened a partnership medical practice in a former rooming house in downtown Colorado Springs, Colorado. The founding physicians and their business manager, who conceived and developed the group, had been professional acquaintances at Northwestern University Medical School and Evanston Hospital in Chicago prior to World War II. Interestingly, none of the original participants had any prior experience in group practice.

The group started in Colorado Springs because the business manager had been stationed at nearby Fort Carson Army Hospital and thought that the town looked like a good place to practice medicine. Members used their GI loan benefits for capital.

At the outset, the physicians met some opposition from the small medical community because of their seemingly unique form of practicing medicine. Further difficulties arose when they were accused of advertising.

The loan to the group had been the first such post-war activity of the Veterans Administration. In seeking visibility, the Veterans Administration notified the *Denver Post* about the formation of the medical center, and the newspaper subsequently published an article entitled, "Trout Stream Lures Doctors to Colorado." This front-page description of the group was not welcomed by the local medical society. One manifestation of the medical community's concern and animosity toward the group was the failure of some individuals to get privileges at one of the local hospitals. Fortunately for the group's early survival, another hospital in town did grant staff privileges to group members.

A second early development that aided the group's survival in what was then a relatively small resort town of 35,000 people was a contract to provide employee health services for a local industry that developed at the end of World War II. Until a few years ago, this contract provided the group physicians with a base income and a ready source of private patients.

In the next decade, both Colorado Springs and the medical center grew rapidly. Growth in the town was a result of tourism, the selection of Colorado Springs as the site for the United States Air Force Academy, and significant federal investments for various military projects in the Colorado Springs area. To meet growing patient demand, a number of physicians were added to the group, and planning began for a new facility. The group's building was opened in January, 1965, in downtown Colorado Springs and is presently still in use: a four-story, 55,000-square-foot facility that cost almost $2 million.

The building has doctors' offices and examining rooms on the periphery; waiting areas and core-service areas in the center; a full radiology suite that provides X-ray and isotope services; a fully equipped clinical laboratory with an SMA-12 auto-analyzer; an optical shop; an opticians' office; a pharmacy; and a physical therapy department.

In 1973, it was estimated that 35,000 people accounted for the year's 101,000 visits to the center, an increase of 10 percent in visits over the previous year. Users of the CSMC are almost exclusively local people who, although they come from all socioeconomic classes, belong primarily to the lower-middle and middle classes. At present, no organized effort is being made to attract a defined patient population; for example, patients are not sent follow-up notices to return for checkups, and outreach programs do not exist. Additionally, although there are now plans under way to survey the clinic's clientele on their usage and opinions about the service, at present little empirical data are available on the group's patients.

Despite the growth and financial success of the group during the second phase of its development, it was obvious that a number of problems existed. A management consultant's report from a public accounting firm in 1960 analyzed the operations of the clinic and pinpointed the following problems:

1. The group essentially functioned as a doctors' office building rather than as a group practice.

2. The group was too democratic; that is, all decisions required a consensus of all partners, which was an impossible dream.

Since the time of that report and a follow-up, a number of major changes have occurred in the way the group organizes itself and makes decisions. In many senses, the group has become somewhat more of a group. This chapter focuses on the activities and relationships of the CSMC in the last several years.

GROUP GOVERNANCE

The present structure of the CSMC dates back to December, 1973, with the signing of the Articles of Partnership. Two classifications of partnership exist: a Class A partner who has full voting privileges; and a Class B partner who is either retired or has, because of lessened professional activity, elected to become a Class B partner. Basically, it is expected that all partners will conduct their entire professional life within the context of the group, and all remuneration received from their professional practice of medicine will go directly into the group's account. The Articles of Partnership allow each Class A partner to have an equal voice in the affairs of the partnership and make provision allowing partners to vote while they are on vacation or out of town.

The executive committee is elected from the partnership and represents the group members in business matters and day-to-day administration. As the partnership agreement sets out:

> All legal instruments shall be made, executed and delivered by the Chairman and Vice Chairman of the Executive Committee, provided that the Executive Committee may from time to time delegate to an administrative officer, director or other designated employee the right, privilege and authority to execute checks, contracts, purchase orders, equipment leases, employment agreements and other routine instruments which are required in the day-to-day operation of the partnership.

The partnership agreement also provides for the addition of new partners, compensation of physicians, and procedures for voluntary and involuntary separation of present partners.

Clearly, the organization's formal power resides in the executive committee, which is made up of eight individuals who serve terms of between two and three years, with the exception of the clinical director, who has an automatic nonvoting appointment for his tenure as director. Members of this committee come from all the specialties, meet once a month, and are compensated at $8 per hour for their services. This minimal compensation is provided because it is expected that they cannot be professionally productive during the course of a meeting. The executive committee's responsibilities and authority cover a range of areas, including personnel, financial, and organizational management. In the area of personnel management, the committee is responsible for the clinic director's evaluation, salary, compensation, and eventually for terminating his tenure and hiring his successor with the approval of the partners.

With regard to other members of the professional staff, the executive committee approves goals and objectives, evaluates professional performance, and approves operating guidelines of professional performance; perhaps most important, it has the authority to take action on behalf of the general partnership for substandard physician performance. Its involvement with the nonprofessional paramedical staff is generally limited to approval of operating performance guidelines and evaluation of employee grievances of a professional nature.

Though the clinic director is generally involved in professional staff recruiting, the executive committee has the responsibility for evaluating and planning staff additions and developing specific standard criteria for new staff, monitoring the recruiting process, and determining compensation for the new staff.

In the area of financial management, the executive committee has the general responsibility for review and approval of professional and nonprofessional compensation packages, as well as the clinic's general financial status. Capital expenditures require the executive committee to "review and approve or disapprove expenditures above $1,000 and under $50,000. If the proposed expenditure will cause the quarterly operating budget to be exceeded by $10,000 or more, the expenditure must be approved by the general Partnership." The committee must also "review and recommend action to be taken by the general Partnership on expenditures over $50,000."

The last area of primary responsiblity for the group is that of organizational management. This involves long-range planning and policy development, such as goal setting, public relations, and major problem solving.

Management in the Group: Two Problems

Like any large, complex organization, Colorado Springs Medical Center has faced a variety of problems in the last several years. Two of these problems are perhaps illustrative of the functions, concerns, and interests of both the group and its management. Additionally, these problems provide a variety of insights into a number of facets of the organization.

Problem 1: Saturday Morning Operation

In November, 1972, a report was issued by the clinic director indicating that a review of the clinic's Saturday morning operations viewed them as a financial drain on the organization. The problem was that the clinic, which was opened and fully staffed from 8:30 A.M. to 1 P.M. every Saturday, did not carry a full patient load during that period but had a limited load made up of walk-ins, many of whom were nonclinic patients. Furthermore, many physicians at the clinic did not see patients on Saturday; the X-ray laboratory, pharmacy, and optical shop were only used in a limited way, and it was expected that further Saturday morning operations would generate an annual loss of almost $22,000.

The executive committee made a series of recommendations to deal with this problem:

1. Continue Saturday operating hours and attempt to reduce employees on Saturday morning in departments which were not productive.

2. Provide minimum services in the laboratory and X-ray departments for Saturday operations.

3. Ask physicians to increase their Saturday appointment loads.

4. Take steps to develop an urgent facility by February 1, 1973.

The follow-up report of January, 1974, indicated that the first two recommendations of the executive committee had been implemented. For example, in the spring and fall of 1972, an average of almost 43 employees were working on any given Saturday; by October, 1973, this number had dropped to 21. However, since the earlier report —and despite the fact that the group had added three physicians since the fall of 1972—the number of doctors coming in on Saturday mornings had dropped from an average of 15 to 11, and the number of patients seen had dropped by about 15 percent. Data indicated that the loss to be expected from the Saturday operations was now estimated to be closer to $20,000, a net decrease of less than $2,000 from the earlier report, despite the fact that the number of employees had been cut by 50 percent. The report of January, 1974, restated the conclusions reached in the earlier report and underscored the need for action on the executive committee's third and fourth recommendations.

In July, 1974, a third report was issued to the group members, again highlighting the problems of the Saturday operation. This report proposed the following alternative solutions:

1. Accept Saturday operations as a financial loss necessitated by the needs of the limited number of patients and physicians; continue "as is" with the entire clinic open, allowing any physician to utilize or not utilize the facility as individually desired.

2. Close the clinic completely on Saturday.

3. Force all physicians to work the clinic on Saturday morning to increase productivity.

4. Provide urgent facilities (for emergency only) on the first floor south wing. This would consist of several examination rooms fully equipped for any reasonable departmental needs, a receptionist to answer phones and schedule patients, nurses with special interest and training in assisting with emergency care, and one or two primary care physicians to field the problems.

5. Provide an urgent care facility as in No. 4, plus several examination rooms for pre-scheduled routine patients, optionally available to any physician located on first floor south wing.

It was the consensus of the executive committee that alternative No. 2 (close down *in toto*) and No. 3 (enforce full Saturday operations) were nonviable; that alternative No. 1 (stay as is) should be pursued if a majority of physicians indicated that preference by active Saturday involvement; otherwise, that alternative No. 4 should be implemented on a trial basis from four to six months, with alternative No. 5 to follow if sufficient physicians demonstrated interest or need.

Problem 2: Medicaid

Following a report from the clinic director in November, 1972, stating that the Colorado Springs Medical Center was losing 23¢ on every dollar charged to Medicaid, with an annual loss of between $70,000 and $100,000, a decision was made to restrict the number of new Medicaid patients. This financial loss was due to several factors. The first was the delayed payment of the Medicaid accounts. The analysis for accounts management at the end of the October billing showed a total of 2,227 Medicaid accounts with an outstanding balance of $188,526, half of which ($93,342) was more than five months old. As a result of this examination, $39,700 was written off.

A second and less serious problem—and one whose financial impact was difficult to analyze—was the fact that an average of 300 Medicaid patients a month either failed to show up or canceled their appointments, precluding the booking of new patients. The administration also identified the Medicaid program as a "costly administrative accounting nightmare." It pointed out that it took three, and sometimes four, clerks to manage the Medicaid accounts, which amounted to the processing of some 12,000 forms per year.

Other problems identified in the report related to a seemingly negative attitude on the part of the staff toward Medicaid patients and a possibility that full-paying patients might resent a heavy Medicaid patient load being handled by the medical center.

The conclusion of the report was as follows:

> Medicaid represents a sizable financial loss to the Center. Medicaid patient load is at least remaining steady, and there is evidence that it is increasing. It is probably the worst single administrative and accounting problem. It is subsidized to the detriment of all concerned except the Medicaid patients themselves. The disproportionate time spent on Medicaid patients, for example, screening, collecting, directing, counseling, et cetera, could be more profitably spent on other patient categories to the greater satisfaction of these patients, and probably to the greater satisfaction of the medical and nonmedical staff.
>
> Much has been made lately of the center's patient relationships. The Medicaid load may be of such disadvantage that it adversely affects the relationship of the center with other patient categories.

A variety of options were envisioned in this report. For example, the center might continue handling Medicaid patients, taking new patients as they came in for appointments. As a second option, they could accept no new patients but continue to service those individuals who had already established a relationship with the center. A third possibility called for a quota system for Medicaid patients. A fourth involved attempting to work with the state welfare offices in order to speed up payments, develop some type of prepaid program, and attempt to develop better overall administrative mechanisms for the program. Finally, the last alternative was simply to phase out the entire Medicaid population and suggest that physicians in the center who wished to care for these people should see them at the city's free clinic on their own time.

Based on this report and on a review of the statistics showing that there were 98 new Medicaid patient registrations per month, a total of 1,076 Medicaid patient visits monthly, and a no-show rate of 28 percent, it was decided to continue services to additional members of Medicaid families who were currently being treated (such as foster or natural children) and to those individuals who go on Medicaid after beginning as fee-for-service patients, but to not accept any other new Medicaid registrants. Within a year, as a result of this policy, the number of new registrations had dropped to an average of 22 per month, and the total visits by Medicaid eligibles had dropped from an average of 1,076 to 472 per month, but the no-show rate had increased by 36 percent.

Further administrative costs were cut by streamlined registration procedures and meetings with state welfare administrators. This resulted in a clinic program of screening Medicaid patients and stamping their claim forms with a certificate of eligibility. This has been of great assistance to both the clinic and Medicaid.

An audit by Medicaid in July, 1973, found that the medical center's operations were 100-percent satisfactory. Nevertheless, the center estimates that it is still losing 28¢ on every Medicaid dollar. But it feels a responsibility to continue handling presently enrolled Medicaid patients.

ATTITUDES OF PHYSICIANS IN THE GROUP

Data for this section came primarily from answers to a written questionnaire conducted by the group's management and completed by 27 of the 28 physicians in 1973.

In general, physicians in the group were positive about many of the aspects of their practice, such as the sense of patient gratitude and support from medical-center employees. On a three-point scale of good, fair, and poor, almost half the physicians indicated that the intellectual challenge, number, type, and source of referrals, and financial remuneration were fair. Almost uniformly, the group felt that there was a high degree of professional and personal compatibility within departments, but that certain areas, such as peer review and professional education, were fair and sometimes poor.

When asked to rate the entire CSMC practice in terms of inter-departmental education, 48 percent indicated that this aspect was poor. Those areas receiving particularly high ratings from the physicians were personal and professional compatibility and group allowance for individuality and business-office management. In addition to the poor rating on interdepartmental education, approximately 25 percent of the group felt that the practice was poorly involved with the community health-planning groups and with the county and state medical societies.

As for change, the group felt that the most pressing needs were for decreasing the overhead and expenses of the group, pursuing the possibility of developing an HMO, establishing satellites, increasing fees, and exploring the possibility of changing the partnership to a professional corporation. Those aspects that were rated least urgent included the expansion of operating hours, the establishment of an acute-care center, and the investigation of a multiphasic screening program.

Turnover within the group is quite low, and, because of the external reputation of the group as well as its location, there is little difficulty in recruiting new members. The following response of a young internist during an interview to a question about why he joined this particular group and what he was looking for, reflects the attitude of many of the young physicians going into this type of group practice:

When I was looking around, Colorado Springs was one of the areas that really was attractive to me, and was attractive both as a place to live and also from the standpoint of my special interest, which is endocrinology. Colorado Springs didn't have anybody who was all that interested in endocrinology, and it looked like a prime setting for me to get established. And, also, the people at Penrose Hospital, the pathology staff there in particular, are really aggressive, forward-looking people with whom I felt confident and could get the sort of laboratory support I needed.

So, in terms of coming to Colorado Springs, that was my justification. As far as going into solo practice or going into group, obviously one of the big features of going into group was having the setup available to handle the business aspects of medicine, which I really don't like to get all that involved in. I'm a lot more comfortable if I don't have to do all that stuff. So that was a feature also. It was a lot more threatening to me then than it is now, because I've learned a little bit about the business of medicine since.

All in all, the group just looked good. I was impressed and pleased with the people in it and the attitudes of the management side of it.

THE MEDICAL CENTER AND THE MEDICAL COMMUNITY

Colorado Springs is a community that is well taken care of in a medical-specialty sense, but according to statistics published by the Comprehensive Health Planning Agency, it has a great lack of primary-care physicians. For example, it was estimated that by 1975 there was a need for 91 general practitioners; in 1977, there were only 30 in the region. In the specialties and subspecialties, however, one sees a rather different picture. For example, at present there are 20 obstetrician-gynecologists, and it is estimated that in the next several years the need will decrease by 4. There are 15 ophthalmologists, and the estimated need is for 9. There are 10 thoracic surgeons, with an estimated need for 20.

Nevertheless, physicians continue to move into Colorado Springs, and there are a variety of active building programs taking place at the various institutions. The largest of these, and some think the best, is Penrose Hospital, which is a 374-bed institution. Penrose is used by the CSMC physicians primarily to hospitalize their medical and surgical patients. Why do they use this hospital as opposed to the other institutions in town? The answer has to do with the nursing staff and the new, excellent facilities that exist at Penrose. The other institution used by a large number of physicians is the 157-bed Memorial Hospital (the old Municipal Hospital), the primary location of the group's obstetrics and pediatrics practice. Group physicians also have privileges at the 157-bed St. Francis Hospital. But they are not involved with either the 101-bed psychiatric hospital, Emory John Brady, or the 122-bed Eisenhower Hospital (which is run for the osteopathic-physician community). Nor is there any significant involvement with the 300-bed Fort Carson Army Hospital or the 135-bed United States Air Force Hospital.

The involvement of the Colorado Springs Medical Center physicians with the medical community, and in particular the hospitals, is quantitatively and qualitatively important. For example, an average of 100 patients per day hospitalized at Penrose Hospital are patients of CSMC physicians. The present chief of staff of Penrose Hospital and the former chief of staff of Memorial Hospital are CSMC members. Does this represent a certain amount of power and leverage for the group? Indeed it does, though in no way does it seem to be exploited.

There are other groups in the area as well, such as several small groups of internists, pediatricians, and general practitioners, and one large doctors' office building where physicians are not grouped. From the hospitals' perspective, these are not really looked upon as groups, but rather as organizations of different physicians with each acting very much as an independent practitioner. Indeed, the notion of the hospital either competing with the group through its own group-practice setup or being captured by a group did not seem to be seriously considered by the hospital administrators or planners, or even by members of the group practice.

PROGRESS AND PROBLEMS

Clearly, the CSMC is in practice for the purpose of providing a stable and viable practice environment for its physicians. The situation for the average doctor in the group is personally and professionally healthy. For example, he has four weeks of annual vacation, two weeks of educational leave, and a variety of fringe benefits, such as a retirement plan and life insurance. Perhaps most important, he is assured of having professional colleagues to cover for him, and, in a sense, he has a built-in referral system.

On the other hand, this particular group has a variety of capitalization problems. For example, it costs each physician $65,000 to buy a share in the realty partnership, which essentially purchases the bricks and mortar of the organization. Upon retirement, this share is refunded to the physician. However, in the past, the funds have been distributed to previous partners; consequently, at the present time, no money exists for retiring individuals.

Also, the young physician entering practice is asking a basic question: Why should he buy $65,000 of bricks and mortar? Perhaps more important, he is unable to get a bank to loan him the $65,000, and the partnership is allowing him to buy as little as $15,000 worth into the organization.

At present, the group is exploring several organizational changes that would reverse their financial situation. One option is to establish a foundation, to which the partnership would sell building and land. Part of the original investment would be returned in cash, and the rest would be a tax-deductible donation to the foundation. The group would then rent space from the foundation and continue its current operations.

Finally, as in private practice, there is a direct link between productivity and income. Typically, a physician will have a base draw somewhere in the neighborhood of $1,500 a month; then, depending upon his personal professional productivity, he can earn as much as $50,000 or $60,000 extra. An interesting sideline is the fact that at the present time a physician can earn productivity "points" not only by his own productivity but also by ordering ancillary services. For example, a pediatrician earns 20¢ on every dollar for laboratory tests that he orders. This system is apparently used in many other group practices, but it is under serious review and will probably be eliminated at the CSMC in the near future.

From the patients' perspective, the medical center offers a wide range of accessible services, continuity of physician management, a pleasant physical environment, and the chance that some quality review will take place. While there is no formal system of quality control within the group, an informal system is imposed by the organizational structure. There are specific standards for group membership. When a patient is seen by a second physician, both charts are reviewed, and the centrally stored unit record is sent to the new doctor. In addition, the pharmacy maintains a patient profile.

Currently, a questionnaire is being developed to ascertain patient attitudes toward the center. Perhaps building the clinic's reputation as a good place to get medical care are innovations such as central billing, the ability to place charges on Master Charge and Bank-Americard, a pharmacy with rates that are competitive with the pharmacies in town, and the convenience and reasonable prices available in the optician's area.

Nevertheless, the clinic's physicians and administrators are worried about the future, and probably rightly so. The goals and objectives of the CSMC were delineated by the chairman of the executive committee in July, 1974, as follows:

In the most general terms the goal of the Colorado Springs Medical Center is to grow from a downtown based primary care facility with sub-specialty support to a significant specialty and sub-specialty referral center serving the community and the southern part of the state, supported by its own primary care referrals based locally.

Current needs necessitate primary attention to financial restructuring in both the Colorado Springs Medical Center and the Medical Center (realty) partnerships. Increased fees, more effective utilization of space and higher physician productivity are the primary methods applicable to CSMC partnership, with greater stability achievable by less fluctuation in physician monthly paychecks and accumulation of an operating reserve. Ultimate conversion from partnership to professional corporation is highly desirable and worth pursuing. The MC partnership will require major changes with more realistic equity evaluation and require urgent liquidation of assets. Ultimate conversion to foundation or sale to third party ownership with retention of physician control seems essential.

In view of the high marketability of primary care and its historic role in Colorado Medical Center operations, professional growth will be initially directed in this area. Methods may include satellite operation, formal/informal association with existing community physicians, implementation of paramedics and multiphasic screening, and/or expansion of industrial medicine input. The addition of a family practice division seems highly desirable. A second professional expansion will then be possible towards specialty and sub-specialty care. Current efforts to augment local and regional referrals are being implemented in addition to encouraging current physicians to practice their specialty capabilities and add new physicians with additional areas of expertise useful to the clinic, community and region. Organizational growth must be achieved by more centralization of benevolent responsive authority in the executive committee, trusted by the partnership, supported by research from the administrative division.

Continuing excellence requires more vigorous ongoing educational efforts, including periodical refresher sabbaticals, informal intradepartmental rounds, interdepartmental conferences, clinical research activities and involvement with a medical school both in Denver and locally. Nonprofessional personnel growth will be directed towards more standardized activities with improved pay, sense of gratification, dialogue with physicians, coordinated supervision and personability to patients. Finally, the clinic must learn how to advertise itself, ethically and agressively.

The future of the group appears bright and the members reflect this optimism. However, the one caution must be that the future will no doubt include changes and new programs, such as National Health Insurance and comprehensive health planning. If the CSMC is to avoid being an anachronism, it must assertively deal with this uncertain future.

COMMENT

The next five years will be critical for the Colorado Springs Medical Center. It is imperative that the group move ahead seriously and vigorously with its satellite operation, since the population of Colorado Springs has moved to the suburbs, where a lack of physicians exists that will be filled by others unless the medical center moves in. Essentially, at the present time the CSMC functions as a primary care group practice with some specialty backup. Its plans are now to develop branch clinics in two suburban areas and staff them on a rotating basis with physicians from the downtown area. Alternatives for the future include moving the entire facility to the suburbs or perhaps maintaining primary care practice in the suburbs and using the downtown clinic as a specialty referral center. Why the push? Obviously, any specialty group needs primary care referrals. Some referrals come from other primary care groups, but, as in all these instances, there is a fear of losing patients.

Furthermore, both Penrose Hospital and Memorial Hospital are aggressively moving ahead to develop doctors' office buildings and perhaps group practices. Neither of these institutions runs what is classically considered an outpatient department, but both provide ancillary services on an ambulatory basis, and both run busy emergency rooms. Penrose's emergency room is staffed by physicians on the Pontiac Plan. (Several of these physicians are CSMC members.) Memorial Hospital, on the other hand, has been handled in a variety of ways. Most recently, a full-time physician was employed as director of the emergency room. He will be hiring and inviting physicians to cover that department. The long-range plans of both of these institutions include a condominium-type doctors' office setup. It appears that the administrators of both these hospitals are primarily interested in having more on-site physicians and, in a sense, centralizing certain aspects of community medical care in their institutions. Indeed, Penrose is seriously considering developing an HMO, which might possibility entice some numbers of the Colorado Springs patient population.

Overall, one gets the sense that Colorado Springs Medical Center is a dynamic organization whose physicians are starting to act and think as a group. As the group grows in size—and everyone agrees that it should and will grow—it is obvious that CSMC must consider a different form of organization and management. For example, the group is beginning to realize that it needs a part-time medical director to assume responsibility for the professional aspects of growth and development. Obviously, this means that each physician would have to devote a portion of working time to paying another physician's salary. No doubt there is physician opposition that must be obviated before such an idea can take solid root. It is equally obvious that administration of such a group requires the skills for nitty-gritty management as well as for long-range planning. The manager must not get caught in the quagmire of the group's everyday aspects and fail to see the changes that are continually occurring in the environment within which the group operates.

Chapter 4

The Brooks Clinic

MIDDLESEX: A CITY IN TRANSITION

The Brooks Clinic is located in Middlesex, a midwestern city with a population of 425,000 that is the major component of a larger population area of one million. Partly due to its central location and solid transportation and industrial base, the city has experienced a 25-percent growth in the past decade.

Suburban Middlesex is characterized by middle and upper middle-class housing areas, good schools, clean industry, little public transportation, and an excellent highway network. The inner city, in contrast, has generally deteriorating formerly middle-class residential neighborhoods, poor schools, adequate public transit, and a downtown business section that is now trying to stem a steady decline with the aid of federal and state redevelopment funds. The population of Middlesex is predominantly white, but since 1960, blacks and other minorities have increased by 20 percent to the point where they now represent a third of the population. The 1970 median family income was $9959 for all racial groups, with blacks and other minorities having an income of $6411.

BROOKS CLINIC: BACKGROUND

The clinic was founded in 1947 at its present location at the edge of the downtown business district and two blocks from St. Luke's Hospital. Two brothers, an internist and a surgeon, opened the practice on the ground floor of their deceased parent's wooden frame home. By 1948, the practice had grown to a size where the Brooks brothers hired on a salaried basis three other physicians: a surgeon who was a distant cousin, and two internists who were former colleagues from the Navy Medical Corps. In 1951, the three employed physicians asked for and received a full partnership in the group. At that time this meant they were no longer salaried, but received an income based on their billings, minus a charge for the office space in the building owned by the Brooks brothers and a prorated share of overhead expenses.

By 1956, the group had grown to eleven partners and a business manager, the former assistant credit manager of Middlesex's largest department store. The frame house, despite renovations, was too small for group efficiency. The solution used was for the group to purchase the house and land from the Brooks brothers and build a totally new clinic building for 18 physicians. By 1965, the group had grown to the 18 physicians and was seeing 45,000 visits per year. Further expansion in 1974 resulted in a building for 30 physician offices and ancillary facilities.

Today's 30 physicians include five internists, one allergist, a cardiologist, an endocronologist, three gastroenterologists, one dermatologist, one neurosurgeon, three pediatricians, two radiologists, five surgeons, one urologist, two orthopedists, one pediatric gastroenterologist, one family physician, and two psychiatrists.

The present mix of physicians was not based on a predetermined recruitment strategy, but resulted from availability of a particular physician at a given time. For example, in 1970 the chief radiologist of the St. Luke's group decided that certain administrative changes at the hospital made practice within that milieu less than satisfactory. So he contacted the radiologist at Brooks, who immediately hired him as assistant radiologist and, after two years, he became a full partner. In the three decades of the group's existence, the turnover of physicians has been low: three salaried doctors left for personal reasons, two because of divorce and subsequent relocation and one because of family illness. Two other doctors left because they failed to be elected to group partnership, and five have retired, including the original founders.

AVAILABILITY AND COST OF CARE

The clinic is open from 8:30 A.M. to 5:30 P.M., Monday through Friday, and 8:30 A.M. to noon on Saturday. Saturday afternoon and Sunday, the clinic is closed, and the availability of any particular physician is a matter of individual scheduling. A patient attempting to locate a physician normally calls the clinic and is advised either to call another physician, stand by for a call back, or go to the St. Luke's emergency room. If patients need to be seen by a clinic physician after hours, they are normally asked to meet the doctor at the St. Luke's emergency room; the clinic is not open for an individual physician to see an individual patient. The availability of any physician during the 48½ hours that the clinic is open is very much at the discretion of the individual physician, since the physician's salary is directly related to his billing plus the preestablished overhead charge. Thus, if physicians desire to work 48 or 49 hours a week, they may. On the other hand, if they wish to reduce their practices, as has occurred several times, doctors may essentially work part time.

Cost of care, however, is on a predetermined basis. For example, an initial workup is $25, all subsequent office visits are $10. There is a fee schedule for operations and for lab and x-ray work, as well as other services, such as physical therapy or vaccination.

QUALITY CONTROL

Most group members feel that the clinic's basic mechanism for quality control is the recruitment of physicians who are Board eligible and have admitting privileges at St. Luke's. The partnership policy established in 1951, and still maintained, is that an employed physician is under review for three years and thereafter eligible for partnership, which must be approved by two-thirds of the existing partners.

At another level, all medical records are centralized, with the exception of those in pediatrics, which are stored within that department. Additionally, the group has a medical utilization review committee, which is nonfunctional.

A final type of informal review occurs when one physician treats a patient of another physician in the practice and the records can be reviewed by the consulting physician. While this may sound conceptually attractive, in fact no one could recall an instance of a referring physician being formally or informally criticized as a result of this type of review.

ORGANIZATION OF THE GROUP

In 1970, one of the senior physicians, Dr. Roger Petersen, emerged as the group's informal leader during the building program. In 1972, the partners awarded him the title of medical director which carried an agreement that he could reduce his practice by 25 percent and he would be reimbursed for his director duties. The medical director is responsible for the planning, quality control, and services delivered by this group. Toward that goal, Dr. Petersen set up a program of continuing education, which includes a weekly luncheon seminar by drug salesmen, an annual continuing education retreat at the clinic, and a $500 travel fund for each clinic member for a maximum of one week's continuing education outside of the Middlesex community.

The drug salesmen symposium format is somewhat unique; drug and equipment salesmen have learned that Wednesday at noon is "show and tell time" at Brooks. They schedule with the business manager a five to ten-minute presentation on their product or drug; after a maximum of four presentations, the physicians can discuss questions with the salesmen. Dr. Petersen believes this is an effective way to produce professional interaction, and also to keep the drug sales representatives away from individual doctors and hence save significant time.

Continuation Education Symposium was started in 1975 and involves a Saturday afternoon, Saturday evening, and all-day Sunday symposium. The group invites two to three local professors from the medical schools, as well as one distinguished visiting professor, to discuss a particular theme. This year's theme was dermatology as a diagnostic tracer. Dr. Lowell Kaplan, a senior distinguished visiting professor from Duke University, spent a weekend at Brooks Clinic, gave a presentation and interacted with the faculty of Middlesex Medical School, and made ambulatory-care service rounds on the two dermatology patients invited in by the clinic dermatologist.

A final element of quality review initiated by Dr. Petersen is the continuing education travel fund for physicians. Most doctors use the $500 to attend general (such as AMA), rather than specialty, professional meetings. Perhaps this trend is best explained by Dr. Petersen in noting that the Middlesex Medical School has a fairly active continuing education program and essentially the Brooks Clinic program is a substitute.

In general, the organization of the group is informal, with the only formal aspect being the six-member board of directors. This board elects a president, a treasurer, and a secretary, and holds periodic meetings. The board's standing committees are the medical records committee, a recruitment committee, and a staff relations committee. Actual day-to-day running is handled by the business manager, as well as the medical director, who meets as *ex officio* board member.

STAFFING

The total staff of the Brooks Clinic is 89, including nurses and technical personnel. At present, no nonphysician paraprofessionals who could substitute for physicians are being used. The idea of using nurse practitioners has been suggested on several occasions; but, the group partners have not felt that this was an appropriate way to deliver medical care. However, the obstetricians are now considering hiring a nurse midwife in lieu of a general duty nurse, and it is expected that this nurse midwife will be providing some patient counseling, prenatal care, and postpartum care.

RELATIONSHIP OF GROUP WITH NEIGHBORING MEDICAL COMMUNITY

The neighboring medical community consists of several voluntary hospitals, a state psychiatric hospital, one proprietary hospital, and a university hospital attached to the Middlesex Medical School. Also, within the next two years, a second state university medical school will be opening in suburban Middlesex. Group members tend to have appointments in at least two hospitals, but most admissions are made to the neighboring St. Luke's Hospital, although the group has no formal relationship with this hospital. However, during the past 20 years, various clinic members have been active on the medical staff of St. Luke's and have held formal positions, including the presidency of the medical board. On any given day, Brooks members are likely to have as many as 65 patients hospitalized at St. Luke's. In order to expedite transfer of information between the hospital and the group, and also to act as an advocate for the group in terms of getting beds or information, the clinic has recently hired an individual to serve as a "hospital secretary" for the Brooks Clinic at St. Luke's Hospital.

The relationship with the medical school is quite good, and various clinic members serve on the school's faculty. Within the last several years, some of the medical school's fulltime faculty have joined the Brooks Clinic as fulltime practitioners, most recently the neurosurgeon. The emergence of the new medical school in Middlesex does represent a potential threat to the Brooks group because of a planned group practice within the medical school. However, members of the Brooks Clinic have individually been active in the planning and development of this new school.

From an administrative perspective, there are no formal relationships with the Health Systems Agency or any of the other health organizations in Middlesex. The Brooks business manager is generally known in the health care community, but he has not been active in local organizations and tends to relate primarily to the Medical Group Management Association for his own professional development.

COMMENT

At first glance, the future appears bright for the Brooks Clinic. They are seeing almost 100,000 visits a year and carry 50,000 active accounts. Patient turnover is low and the physicians appear to be satisfied as members of a group.

However, in the last decade, due to the deteriorating situation in downtown Middlesex, many patients are forced to drive from the suburbs to see their doctors. There has been some talk about the group either opening a second office in the suburban area or perhaps relocating the entire clinic in the suburbs. However, there has yet to be any formal marketing analysis of the patients, their needs, their usage patterns, living areas, and so forth.

Part of the reason for a reluctance to move to the suburbs is a potential conflict with the new medical school's group. It is felt that the new medical school, with its physicians' practice plans, may represent far more complications for the Brooks Clinic than presently exist in downtown Middlesex.

It should be recognized that the clinic basically encompasses three separate operations. First is the partnership of physicians, who are in the business of delivering medical care. The only members are physicians who are formally elected into partnership and have organized themselves with a Board of Directors. The second organization is a land and building corporation, which owns the land and premises of the Brooks Clinic, and rents the land to the partnership. Individual partners when they join the group must put up a $10,000 bond in order to become a partner in the building corporation. This corporation is set up with full and limited partners, including the group's business manager, who is a member of the partnership. The third corporation owns the equipment in the building and leases the equipment to the partnership. This corporation is also set up with its own board and membership, and includes nonphysicians as well as physicians.

In sum, the Brooks Clinic is typical of a medium-sized, private, for-profit group practice that has grown and flourished without any strategic planning and still remains, in many senses, an immature organization. It has for the last two decades been a growth industy; indeed, it is difficult to envision the Brooks Clinic ever failing. Yet there are dramatic changes ahead, including new and more prestigious competition, a disadvantageous physical location, and a series of disorganized relationships with other providers that have the potential for leaving various group members out in the cold.

What can be done? Perhaps the first and most important step is to realize that the clinic may be heading into troubled times. This should result in an immediate assessment of the clinic's strengths and weaknesses, and the opportunities and constraints in Middlesex, as well as the options available for the group in other forms, such as a merger between St. Luke's and Brooks.

However, as is obvious in this case, the group's analysis of the future is such that they are disinterested in any program that will impinge on their practice. Thus, Brooks Clinic has continued to carry on business as usual, while disregarding possible future difficulties. The management tends to be efficient, but it does not appear to be taking as aggressive a role as it is probable capable of.

Chapter 5

The Sunset Medical Group, P.C.

William P. Ferretti *

THE SUNSET MEDICAL GROUP, P.C.

In late March of 1974, Dr. Andrew Terry and Dr. Laurence Eljay became concerned about their practice, the Sunset Medical Group, P.C., a private family practice.

"Larry, I still think we did the right thing when we closed the practice to new patients," said Dr. Terry. "I know the people in the community are unhappy, but we simply can't handle any more new patients. We haven't taken any vacations or time off for educational meetings, and I can't remember the last time either of us has been home for supper on a week night."

Somewhat wearily, Dr. Eljay replied, "I don't know what to do, Andy. Obviously we need a third physician, but we aren't making enough to pay ourselves, let alone a new guy. We're damned if we do and damned if we don't."

Dr. Terry nodded. "That's what gripes me—all this hard work might be worthwhile if our heads were above water. But this new practice has been a nightmare. We're both drawing smaller salaries than we did in our old practice, and it seems like we spend more time talking to bankers about loans than we do caring for our patients. Also it looks like when April 30th rolls around, we'll be in the red."

When Drs. Terry and Eljay dissolved their partnership in Lincoln, New York, and organized a professional corporation in nearby Caldwell, they expected their practice to change, and they expected the change to be beneficial to the community and to themselves.

---

* Mr. Ferretti is presently the Executive Director of the Dorothy Rider Pool Health Care Trust in Allentown, Pennsylvania.

DEVELOPMENT OF THE SUNSET MEDICAL GROUP

Sunset had not only been preceded by the partnership of Drs. Terry and Eljay, but by two other practices as well. The original practice had been organized by Dr. Paul Dell as a solo practice in his home in Lincoln and was taken over by Dr. Terry, who continued to operate it as a solo practice for two years until Dr. Eljay's arrival. This third practice operated for nearly two years as a partnership until May, 1973, when the SMG was formed, and Drs. Terry and Eljay moved from the office in Dr. Terry's Lincoln home to a new, leased facility in Caldwell.

When Dr. Dell opened the practice in 1961, he did not become active until after the death of an older established physician in the community. Dr. Dell had office hours four and one-half days a week and three evenings. Emergencies were treated on Saturdays, a limited number of house calls made, daily hospital rounds conducted, obstetrical services offered for the first five years, nursing home patients followed, and school health services offered at the Regional High School one afternoon each week. In addition, Dr. Dell served as the Deputy County Physician. In the last few years of practice, Dr. Dell grossed over $50,000, which provided annual net incomes in the high $30s and low $40s.

In 1969, Dr. Terry spent one-half day a week moonlighting in Dr. Dell's office during the last year of his residency at the Tazwell Hospital in Richlands. During that year, Dr. Dell decided to accept a faculty position at the State University Medical School. Consequently, Dr. Terry took over the practice in July of 1969, and Dr. Dell left six weeks later. Prior to leaving, Dr. Dell sent notices to 2,000 families representing approximately 6,000 of his patients. The practice Dr. Dell left was limited to the rapidly growing immediate geographic area.

In the two ensuing years, Dr. Terry aggressively sought to expand the practice so that he could attract a partner. He accepted new patients from outside the immediate geographical area, added two elementary schools to his school health responsibilities, and continued to make house calls.

Meanwhile, in the fall of 1969 shortly after his entry into the Navy, Dr. Eljay began to discuss forming a practice with Dr. William Fredericks, who had been one year behind Dr. Eljay in the residency program at Tazwell Hospital. It was tentatively agreed that Dr. Eljay would form a solo practice upon discharge from the Navy in 1971, and that Dr. Fredericks would join him to form a partnership upon his discharge from the Army in 1972. When Dr. Terry learned of the plans of Drs. Eljay and Fredericks, he offered to form a three-member group practice.

In August, 1971, the partnership was formed with Drs. Terry and Eljay. The office in Dr. Terry's home was too small for two physicians, for it only had two examining rooms and one consultation room. As a result, Drs. Terry and Eljay approached a local businessman, Mr. Robert Peterson, and encouraged him to build a new facility which they would lease. It was decided that the ideal site would be in Caldwell on Route 49, two miles from the intersection of the new interstate highway. Drs. Terry and Eljay recognized that additional space would be needed both to attract Dr. Fredericks and to operate more efficiently. Moreover, the new facility would allow them to provide additional services presently not offered, such as EKG's, proctoscopy examinations, laboratory services, and audiometry testing.

It was originally anticipated that the building would be contructed by the summer of 1972, when Dr. Fredericks was due to be discharged from the Army. Despite the fact that the construction had not been completed by July, Dr. Fredericks purchased a home in Richlands. However, he was only able to work in the Lincoln practice for six weeks that summer when Drs. Terry and Eljay were on vacation because of the lack of space. Ultimately, Dr. Fredericks grew impatient and decided to form his own solo practice in Richlands, and built an office addition to his home.

The Caldwell facility was finally completed in May of 1973, and Drs. Terry and Eljay formed a professional corporation, the Sunset Medical Group, P.C. The corporate form of organization was chosen for three principal reasons:

1. It would permit them to tax shelter anticipated increases in income by using the additional income to purchase benefits, such as a retirement plan and life and health insurance for corporation members, using corporate funds.

2. Formation of the corporation would allow Drs. Terry and Eljay to increase their below-average fees in spite of the wage and price restraints of the Economic Stabilization Program.

3. Since the practice was moving into a new location, it seemed an opportune time to reinforce the practice's new identity.

SIZE OF THE SUNSET MEDICAL GROUP

The original service area of the partnership practice of Drs. Terry and Eljay included Cabotsville, Cadburry, Caldwell, Lincoln, and Jefferson. This area, according to the 1970 census, had a total population of 12,951. The primary service area* of the SMG included the above-mentioned communities, as well as Beecham, Hollis, Humphreys, and Twin Oaks, whose population totaled 9,210 people, for a grand total of 22,161.

An analysis of the population growth in those communities (Table 5-1) revealed an overall population increase of 34.7 percent in the time period between 1960 and 1970. Moreover, by 1975 the population was expected to exceed 25,000 people for an increase of 14.7 percent. This factor alone accounted for a dramatic increase in the physician-to-population ratio in SMG service area. In addition to this population increase, there had been a decrease in the supply of physicians serving these communities. In 1974, the only other practicing physicians in the SMG service area were Dr. Pike in Caldwell, Dr. McCutcheon in Humphreys, and Dr. Finland in Twin Oaks. In the last three years between 1971 and 1974, the communities of Cabotsville, Caldwell, Hollis, and Prichardville (which is part of Caldwell) lost four physicians due to retirement, death, and a leave of absence, thereby halving the available supply of physicians. Accordingly, using 1970 population figures, the physician-to-population ratio had increased from one physician to 2,770, to one physician to 5,540. If the increase in population since 1970 were taken into account, the physician-to-population ratio would undoubtedly exceed one physician to 6,000.

An actual count of the family medical records at SMG when the practice was closed to new patients in October, 1973, indicated that SMG was caring for approximately 3,800 families. By the spring of 1974, a more current figure would undoubtedly have been in the range of 4,000 families, for a total of approximately 12,000 patients, assuming an average family size of three people.

Unfortunately, Drs. Terry and Eljay did not keep monthly service statistics, so that it was difficult to estimate the number of patient visits delivered. Statistics were kept, however, for the month of March, 1974, and resulted in a total of 1,617 outpatient visits. If this were an average figure, the practice would have been delivering in

---

* SMG served patients from throughout the county and outside the county as well, but the primary service area represented the source of most patients.

excess of 19,000 outpatient visits per year. Until the practice closed its doors to new patients, it was growing at the rate of 100 new patients each week; and since this closing, approximately 50 patients were being turned away each week.

Table 5-1

Population of the Service Area of the
Sunset Medical Group, 1960-1975*

	1960	1970	Percentage Increase 1960-1970	(Projected)*	Percentage Increase 1970-1975
Cabotsville	777	970	24.8%	1,080	11.3%
Cadburry	1,159	1,742	50.4%	2,050	17.7%
Caldwell	3,770	5,119	35.8%	6,200	21.1%
Lincoln	880	885	0.6%	990	11.9%
Jefferson	2,841	4,235	49.1%	4,900	15.7%
	9,427	12,951	37.4%	15,220	17.5%
Beechman	1,090	1,385	27.1%	1,540	11.2%
Gardner	787	874	11.1%	920	5.3%
Hollis	1,135	1,386	22.1%	1,480	6.8%
Humphreys	2,148	2,606	21.3%	2,840	9.0%
Twin Oaks	1,908	2,959	55.1%	3,410	15.2%
	7,068	9,210	30.3%	10,190	10.6%
TOTAL	16,495	22,161	34.7%	25,411	14.7%

* Source: Tazwell County Planning Board

SERVICES PROVIDED

The practice was open five days a week, with office hours from 9:00 a.m. to noon and from 1:00 p.m. until 5:00 p.m., with one physician seeing patients in the morning, and both physicians seeing patients on Monday, Tuesday, and Friday afternoons. In addition, SMG had evening office hours from 7:00 p.m. until approximately 10:00 p.m., with both physicians on Monday and Tuesday evenings and one physician on Wednesday and Thursday evenings. Moreover, one physician took emergency and after-hours calls 24 hours a day, 7 days a week, with Drs. Terry and Eljay alternating weekend coverage of the inpatients and rotating outpatient coverage every fourth weekend with Drs. Pike and Finland.

Patients or families were encouraged to receive all or most of their primary care from either Dr. Terry or Dr. Eljay. Accordingly, the medical records were centrally stored, with a folder for each family and individual progress sheets for family members. The simple medical records systems, used since Dr. Terry's original practice, consisted of manila file folders with loosely stored material.

A written preventive medicine protocol for males over 40 years old had been developed, and a similar protocol had been developed for well babies, although it was not in writing. Female patients were urged to obtain appointments for annual Pap smears, but a reminder recall system had not been developed. Drs. Terry and Eljay had expressed interest in developing a nurse protocol for diabetes and hypertension follow-up visits, but had not found time to do so. Drs. Terry and Eljay also lacked the time to teach their diabetic patients and other chronic disease patients about their illnesses, although they did adequately cover topics such as breast self-examination and accident prevention for children.

Basic laboratory procedures such as urinalysis, hematocrits, and cultures were performed at SMG; most other laboratory work was sent to the Plattsburg Medical Lab, which billed SMG, which in turn billed patients. SMG also performed EKG testing and audiometry testing.

Drs. Terry and Eljay maintained admitting privileges exclusively at the Tazwell Hospital and admitted nearly all of their patients to Tazwell. Drs. Terry and Eljay did not offer obstetrical services, and referred other patients requiring specialty services to physicians on the staff of the Tazwell Hospital. Some patients requiring super-specialty care were sent to major medical centers in Albany or New York City.

Inpatient care of SMG patients was rendered by the "rounder," who alternated coverage of inpatients one week at a time and conducted daily rounds from 9:00 a.m. until noon. SMG had an estimated average daily census of six patients at Tazwell, and morning rounds generally took three hours, especially for new admissions. Sometimes the rounder would see a SMG patient who was sent directly to the emergency room or to the hospital for emergency laboratory or x-ray work. If time permitted, the rounder also made social calls on SMG patients admitted to specialty services.

All patients requiring nursing home care were admitted to the Longwood Nursing Home located nearly equidistant between SMG and the hospital on Route 49. SMG maintained an average daily census at Longwood of six patients. Before the practice was closed to new patients in October of 1973, the average daily census was nearly double. When problems with SMG patients arose at Longwood, attempts were usually made to have the patient seen by the rounder. Otherwise, responsibility for conducting routine visits one Friday a month from 1:00 to 3:00 p.m. at Longwood was alternated between Drs. Terry and Eljay. In addition, SMG cared for patients from Norton's Guest Home and Amy's Rest Home, all of whom were seen in the office.

Approximately two house calls were made each week, generally for elderly and disabled patients. The responsibility for making house calls was not alternated between the two physicians. Instead, patients were assigned to each physician on a geographical basis; that is, the patients were seen by the physician who lived nearest to their home. House calls were usually made by the physician on Tuesday and Friday afternoons, and occasionally one of the nurses from SMG made the house call when only an injection was required.

Limited use was made of the Visiting Nurse Association, for Drs. Terry and Eljay felt the families were independent and managed to care for their own family members. When dealing with complex social and family problems, SMG utilized the services of the hospital's Social Service Department, local school child study teams, and the State's Bureau of Children's Services.

SMG maintained contracts with the North Tazwell Regional High School and four elementary schools. The high school contract required coverage of football games, visits on Tuesday afternoons from 1:00 to 3:00 p.m., when athletic physical examinations were conducted and athletic and school-related problems seen. A large number of the estimated 2,000 physical examinations a year were conducted on the first few Saturdays each fall. SMG received $3,000 for this service.

At the four elementary schools, physical examinations were performed and reviews made of the screening tests performed by the school nurses (hearing, TB, etc.). Visits to schools were on Friday afternoons, from September to January, or until the physical examinations had been completed. SMG received $400 for its contract with the Lincoln Elementary School, $150 from the Jefferson Elementary School, and $200 each from the Cabotsville and Gardner Elementary Schools.

APPOINTMENT SYSTEM

After SMG closed its practice to new families, only regular patients were given appointments to be seen by Dr. Terry or Dr. Eljay. The waiting time for a routine visit was six to eight weeks.

SMG maintained four incoming telephone lines, two of which were unlisted and used by pharmacies, by other physicians, and by the telephone company (for emergency use). A one-week sample of incoming telephone calls on the two listed phone lines resulted in an average of 98 incoming calls between 9:00 a.m. and 6:00 p.m. It was estimated that at least as many outgoing calls were made each day. As a result of this large volume of calls, a number of patients were put on hold for long periods of time. On Monday and Tuesday mornings, two employees were responsible for receiving incoming calls; at other times one person was assigned to incoming telephone lines. At 11:00 a.m., 3:00 p.m., and 6:00 p.m., the person responsible for telephone duty shifted to another job, so that nearly all of the staff at SMG shared telephone duty. On Monday through Thursday, phone lines were switched over to the answering service from 6:00 p.m. until 9:00 a.m. the following morning. On Friday, the lines were switched over to the answering service at 3:00 p.m. because of the large number of people who tried to receive appointments prior to the weekend.

Although time was not blocked out for emergencies, patients with bona fide emergencies were told to come to the office immediately and were seen at once. Patients with urgent problems, however, encountered greater difficulty in being seen. Patients with an urgent complaint were told to recite their problem, which was noted on a self-sticking note pad that was placed on the patient's progress sheet in the medical record folder. The patient was then told to stand by and await a return telephone call. Each patient's problem was then reviewed by one of the physicians at 11:00 a.m., 3:00 p.m. or 6:00 p.m., at which time telephone duty was switched. Then the employee going off telephone duty called each of the patients back and either offered an evening appointment or some other disposition, such as a prescription. It is estimated that 80 percent of the requests for appointments were reviewed by physicians in the above manner.

Reappointments were made as part of the routine patient visit process. The system began prior to the patient's visit, when the patient's medical record was pulled out of the file. When the patient arrived, a peg log voucher slip was attached to the chart, and the chart was placed in the passthrough into the nurse's station. The patient was then escorted into an examining room, where intake data was charted by the nurse or medical assistant, and the chart was placed on the door. After the patient was seen by the physician and other ancillary services were provided (e.g., lab, EKG, injection, etc.), the physician marked the voucher slip with the charge and noted when a reappointment would be needed, if at all. The patient was then escorted to the reception desk, and the chart was left to be filed.

Patients sometimes were told by the doctors to drop in at their convenience within a week or so for blood pressure checks, injections or various follow-up services requiring that they be seen only by the nurse or medical assistant.

PRACTICE ORGANIZATION AND MANAGEMENT

Drs. Terry and Eljay were the only officers of the Sunset Medical Group, P.C. and served as president and secretary-treasurer, respectively. SMG was served by a tax lawyer, an insurance consultant, and an accountant.

All employees at SMG reported directly to both Drs. Terry and Eljay, and no supervisory authority was formally delegated to any employee. Both Drs. Terry and Eljay wrote checks and made credit decisions. Their only formal contact to discuss practice management was on alternate Friday evenings when the payroll checks were drawn.

Personnel Management

SMG employed two full-time and seven part-time employees, including four R.N.'s, two medical assistants, one file clerk, one bookkeeper, and one insurance clerk. This large staff allowed for readily available vacation and sick time coverage. Employee staffing hours in some cases had not changed since Dr. Dell's practice. Current employee staffing hours are outlined in Table 5-2.

Table 5-2
Sunset Medical Group, P.C., Staffing Hours

- R.N.: Approximately 34 hours a week—8:30 a.m.-5:00 p.m., Monday-Thursday.

- R.N.: Approximately 34 hours per week—8:30 a.m.-5:00 p.m., Monday, Wednesday, Friday, and 1:00 p.m. to 10:00 p.m. or closing, Thursday.

- R.N.: Approximately 24 hours per week—4:00 p.m. to 10:00 p.m. or closing, Monday, Tuesday, Wednesday.

- R.N.: Approximately 8 hours a week—10:00 a.m. to 6:00 p.m. on Saturday.

- Medical Assistant: Approximately 36 hours per week—9:00 a.m. to 6:00 p.m., Monday; 1:00 p.m. to 10:00 p.m. or closing, Tuesday, Wednesday, Thursday.

- Medical Assistant: Approximately 45 hours per week—1:00 p.m. to 10:00 p.m. or closing, Monday; 8:00 a.m. to 5:00 p.m., Tuesday, Wednesday, Thursday, Friday.

- File Clerk: Approximately 33 hours per week—8:30 a.m. to 3:00 p.m., Monday through Friday.

- Bookkeeper: Approximately 30 hours per week—9:00 a.m. to 3:00 p.m., Monday through Friday.

- Insurance Clerk: Approximately 20 hours per week—1:00 p.m. to 4:00 p.m., Monday; 9:00 a.m. to 4:00 p.m. Tuesday; 7:00 p.m. to 10:00 p.m. or closing, Wednesday; Noon to 6:00 p.m. Friday.

Facilities Management

The building occupied by SMG was completed in the spring of 1973, using modular construction methods. The 3,109 square feet of office space were rented to SMG by Mr. Peterson for a negotiated figure of $600 a month.

Originally, it had been expected that the monthly rental figure would be much higher. Drs. Terry and Eljay, however, were so distressed at the additional time that was taken to complete the building and at the subsequent loss of Dr. Fredericks, that they threatened to keep their practice in Dr. Terry's home unless the rental figure was lowered. Mr. Peterson was encountering cash flow problems of his own and quickly realized that he could not readily rent the space, so he agreed to the negotiated rental figure.

The facility (Figure 5-1), which had been designed for three to four physicians, included adequate parking, a large waiting room, a reception area, medical records storage space, a large nurses' station with laboratory equipment, ten examination rooms, a large room with desks and book shelves for three physicians, a combination business office and conference room, a staff lounge and kitchen, utility rooms, and a large basement.

Figure 5-1

Floor Plan of the Sunset Medical Group, P.C.

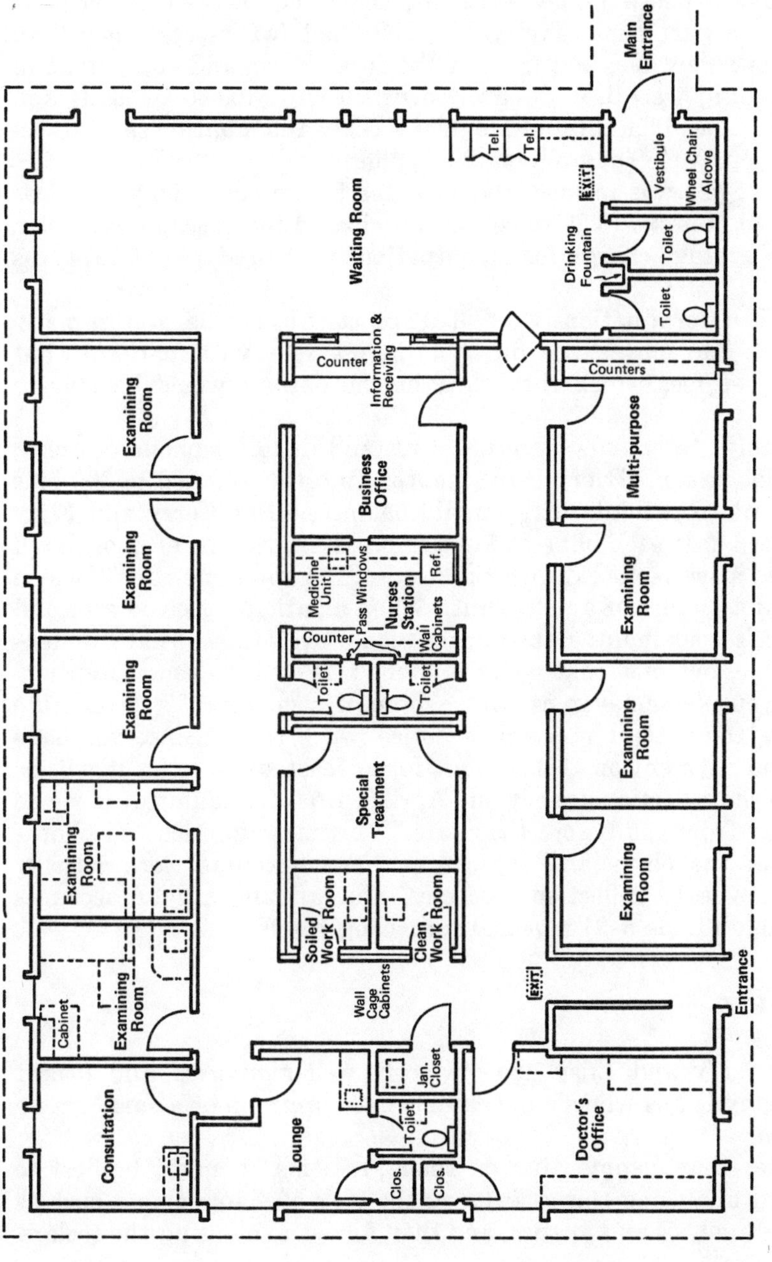

Financial Management

At the end of the fiscal year ending April 30, 1974, SMG generated less than $150,000 in revenue and incurred a deficit of nearly $12,000. The major expense item was the $62,000 payroll for the two full-time and seven part-time employees. SMG had few assets other than accounts receivable, and most of the furnishings and equipment in the building were leased. SMG owed nearly $10,000 in loans and notes payable, in addition to regular weekly and monthly short-term accounts payable (payroll, taxes, suppliers, etc.).

When SMG was formed, the basic fee for an outpatient visit was increased from $6 to $9 to reflect anticipated increases in overhead, yet the average charge for an outpatient visit in March of 1974 was $7.58.

Credit determinations were made by the physicians, and in many instances the physicians did not discuss fees with patients, but merely set fees which they thought the patient would be able to afford.

Monthly statements were not sent, and little telephone dunning was undertaken. Every three months an estimated 200 to 300 bills were sent to patients with unpaid balances. Drs. Terry and Eljay estimated that each bill cost $1.50 to process. Each three-month bill included a stick-on seal with the words, "Did you remember?" which also had a picture of an elephant. When a patient received a second notice after six months, the sticker read, "Overlooked! That's under-standable, but now that we've brought this item to your attention, won't you please favor us with a prompt remittance?" After nine months, the patient was sent a notice which read, "Since you have made no payment on this account for at least six months, it will be sent to the collection agency on [April 8, 1974, for example] if we do not hear from you before that date." This message included photo-copies of the physicians' signatures. Few accounts were actually turned over to collection agencies, and an analysis of accounts receivable (Table 5-3) revealed surprising results.

COMMENT

Drs. Terry and Eljay are obviously well-motivated and bright young physicians who simply cannot make a group of a small group practice.

Rather than commenting on their problems, it might be best to begin by analyzing this case, using the tools of management such as systems analysis and finance, and then follow up by using the tools of public health such as epidemiology and biostatistics. Then a synthesis of these disciplines should be made. Hopefully, the result will provide a workable plan for the future.

Table 5-3

Accounts Receivable Analysis, Sunset Medical Group, P.C.

	Charges	Collections	Month End Accounts Receivable	Days Outstanding Accounts Receivable		
May 1973	$12,981	$ 9,027	$ 3,891	$ 3,891	=	6.6 days
22 days	$ 587/day	$ 410/day	$ 177/day	$ 587		
Aug. 1973	$12,440	$10,834	$10,619	$10,619	=	19.6 days
23 days	$ 540/day	$ 471/day	$ 462/day	$ 541		
Dec. 1973	$10,013	$ 9,649	$13,939	$13,939	=	26.4 days
19 days	$ 527/day	$ 508/day	$ 734/day	$ 527		
Mar. 1973	$13,903	$13,373	$16,045	$16,045	=	24.2 days
21 days	$ 662/day	$ 637/day	$ 764/day	$ 662		

Exhibit 5-1

Tasks and Duties of Nurses and Medical Assistants

1. Telephone Responsibilities

   a. Receive requests for appointments
   b. Obtain appointment decisions from physicians
   c. Call back patients
   d. Make appointments for RMG patients at HMC departments

2. Patient Care Related Activities

   a. Blood pressure checks
   b. Set up examining rooms
   c. Obtain brief history and description of patient's complaints
   d. Chaperone
   e. Perform surgical preps
   f. Suture removal
   g. Dressing changes
   h. Injections
   i. Obtain lab specimens (i.e., throat cultures, blood drawing, etc.)

Exhibit 5-1 Continued

3. Other Activities

    a. Equipment maintenance
    b. Ordering supplies
    c. Autoclave
    d. Tracking lab reports
    e. Seeing detail men
    f. Blocking out appointment book*

Exhibit 5-2

Tasks and Duties of File Clerk

1. Filing loose material
2. Pulling charts for next day's visits and for telephone calls
3. Filing charts
4. Signing patients in and out
5. Collecting money
6. Emptying trash
7. Maintaining supply of soap and paper products

Exhibit 5-3

Tasks and Duties of Bookkeeper

1. Maintain daily ledger
2. Monitor accounts receivables
3. Mail bills
4. Perform daily banking chores
5. Pick up mail at post office
6. Sign patients in and out
7. Collect money
8. Process Medicare and Medicaid forms
9. Perform some typing

---

*This duty performed by only one of the staff members.

Exhibit 5-4

Tasks and Duties of Insurance Clerk

1. Process insurance forms
2. Mail bills
3. Handle all telephone-related responsibilities
4. Perform blood pressure checks
5. Set up examination rooms
6. Record patient complaint and brief history
7. Chaperone

Exhibit 5-5

Balance Sheet as of April 30, 1974
Sunset Medical Group, P.C.

Cash in Bank		($ 2,946)
Cash on Hand		172
Current Assets		($ 2,774)
Fixed Assets		$ 1,934
Intangible Assets	$2,500	
Less Accumulated Amortization	- 500	2,000
Total Assets		$ 1,160
Salaries and Wages Payable		$ 4,841
Short-Term Notes		4,084
Current Liabilities		$ 8,925
Long-Term Debt		$ 5,868
Common Stock		200
Capital Surplus		165
Retained Earnings		(13,998)
Total Liabilities & Net Worth		$ 1,160

Exhibit 5-6

Retained Earnings Statement
as of April 30, 1974
Sunset Medical Group, P.C.

Retained Earnings May 1, 1973	0
Net Income April 30, 1974	($11,644)
Expense Not Deducted (Buy-Sell Insurance)	($ 2,354)
Retained Earnings April 30, 1974	($13,998)

Exhibit 5-7

Income and Expense Statement
Fiscal Year Ending April 30, 1974
Sunset Medical Group, P.C.

Revenue	$146,014
Expenses	
Physicians' Salaries & Wages	43,050
Other Salaries & Wages	62,111
Fringe Benefits	3,498
F.I.C.A.	3,809
Unemployment Compensation Insurance	2,000
Medical & Surgical Supplies	8,778
Other Supplies & Expenses	3,481
Leased Equipment	3,679
Laboratory Fees Paid to Philadelphia Medical Lab	2,824
Depreciation Medical & Surgical Equipment	195
Depreciation Office Equipment	159
Amortization Organization Expense	500
Leased Facilities	7,200
Maintenance	142
Contract Housekeeping	1,778
Telephone	3,721
Utilities	2,697
Cash Short	353
Travel	0
Dues	1,025
Entertainment	350
Charity	121
Professional Fees	4,992
License Fees	75
Collection Fees	155
Miscellaneous	308
Interest	651
Personal Property Taxes	6
Total Expenses	$157,658
Net Income (Loss)	($ 11,644)

Part II
Hospital-Based Ambulatory Care

Chapter 6

Hospital-Based Ambulatory Care: A Critical Assessment

One of the many proffered solutions for the various economic and social problems plaguing the health system is that of expanding the network of hospital-based ambulatory care programs. Proponents of such expansion argue that it is the next natural developmental stage for the system because consumers are increasingly becoming unable to make the appropriate connections with medical practitioners and are turning to the thousands of generally well-distributed and located community hospitals as their primary source of all medical care.

Those who are negative about more hospital-based ambulatory care programs argue that hospitals are the most expensive, inefficient, and poorly managed components of the health system—why give them something else to foul up?

Polemics, and perhaps reason, aside, a major commitment has been made to a variety of hospital-based ambulatory care by the government through some parts of such developmental programs as Hill-Burton, Health Maintenance Organizations, and even categorical grants, such as the Maternal and Infant Care and Children and Youth Projects. Private philanthropy is also active, most recently and notably the Robert Wood Johnson Foundation, which is in the process of awarding $30 million to hospitals for the development of hospital-based primary care group practices.

The size and potential significance of this investment for restructuring the health system suggests that consideration be given to a variety of questions, including the following: How are consumers utilizing their various ambulatory care options? How do physicians fit into the hospital-based ambulatory care puzzle? And finally, what problems are hospitals facing in their ambulatory care programs—and why?

This discussion and analysis of the foregoing questions is based on literature review, numerous meetings and interviews with consumers, planners and administrators of ambulatory care programs, and 36 field visits made in conjunction with an 18-month study of community hospital-based primary care programs.

CONSUMER USE OF AMBULATORY CARE OPTIONS

Consumers of health services have basically three ambulatory care options open to them: the doctor's office, a hospital clinic or a hospital emergency room.

Recent preliminary data from the national Ambulatory Medical Care Survey indicate that on the average there are 3.1 office-based physician visits per year per person. [1] This data closely corresponds with the previously available information from the National Center for Health Statistics which indicated that there were approximately 4.9 physician visits per person per year, of which 69.6 percent or 3.4 physician visits per year per person were to office-based physicians. [2] Although the number of physician visits per year has increased slightly per year, these increases appear to be more related to the collection methodology than to significant changes in consumer ambulatory use patterns.

A different picture is seen when one looks at the experiences hospitals have had in their outpatient clinics and emergency rooms. For example, in 1964, hospitals reported a total of 125 million outpatient visits; a decade later the number had more than doubled to over 250 million visits. Further, this occurred at a time when the national population had increased by 20 percent, outpatient departments had become deficit operations, the number of physicians was increasing, and the number of hospitals with outpatient clinics declining. Simultaneously, emergency department visits increased at an even greater rate. In 1964, there were 26 million emergency department visits, and by 1974 the total had mushroomed to over 71 million visits. Perhaps of greater significance are various studies indicating that a majority of the emergency department patients are utilizing that facility for primary care.[3, 4]

Although the statistics are helpful for getting a handle on the parameters of the ambulatory care problem, we are still faced with the basic dilemma—why is this happening? Several explanations seem reasonable. First, a large segment of the population is highly mobile. Illustrating this is the data from the U.S. Census which found that about 37 percent of the population had moved from one house to another between 1970 and 1974.[5] No doubt many of these moves require the establishment of a new relationship with a medical practitioner—and in some instances the hospital's OPD and ER become a temporary or permanent substitute for such relationships. Perhaps marketers of HMOs should take advantage of this mobility and its accompanying uncertainty and sell their plans through moving companies and welcome wagon agencies.

A second explanation is that physicians are encouraging their patients to use the ER during off hours. A cynic might note this is the way for physicians to insure patients high quality and readily available care that is not physically draining on themselves and represents little risk of loosing his patient. Indeed, hospital use offers doctors many of the advantages of group practice with few of the risks. For example, M.C. Olendzki reports that

> the phenomenon of the hospital covering or substituting for the private physician, or acting as an extension of his private office (the "meet me's") is extremely widespread and accounts for a large volume of ES visits. It occurs with almost identical frequency in hospitals with OPD's and in those without; and it is reported especially in voluntary hospitals, in those of medium to fairly large bed size, and in communities of intermediate size.[6]

A third common observation from field experiences is that patients using the ER and OPD had a "womb" feeling toward those organizations; that is, they felt that once they were inside the hospital, they would be taken care of. Although a fair number of complaints were heard about waiting time for care, few people were observed to leave the emergency room to seek care elsewhere, such as at a private practitioner's office (although people often left OPDs to get care at a hospital's ER).

A final observation is related to the economics of ambulatory care. In the past decade we have witnessed the development of a number of health care programs which, while having the intent of eliminating the financial barriers to ambulatory care, have to a major extent not changed many of the patterns of ambulatory care usage. Indeed, few hospital OPDs have suffered dramatic patient losses as a result of the implementation of Medicare or Medicaid.

PHYSICIANS AND AMBULATORY CARE

What has been observed over the past decade is the movement of greater numbers of physicians into hospital and group-related ambulatory care practices that range from highly organized hospital-based primary care group practices to loose-knit medical arts buildings proximate to hospitals. The important question to consider in this section is: What is behind this movement? A variety of explanations can and have been offered. Perhaps the most popular is that physicians are economic beings who realize that, with the exception of super specialists, most medicine is ambulatory care and the most efficient and personally economical way to practice it is in a group situation. Such a situation usually requires a minimal capital investment, has a certain stability which is attractive to a fledging physician, and offers future earning and pension benefits. These, together, seem to satisfy short, medium and long-range goals of many practitioners.

Two other not previously identified explanations for this movement toward hospital and group-related ambulatory care practice are: (a) the practitioner role of the medical educator or "role model" has shifted, with an obvious resultant shift in the student, and (b) the movement is a logical and anticipated consequence of the traditional values of medicine.

Support of the first explanation comes from the observation that in the past decade a significant number of medical schools have developed some sort of physician practice plan that has included a group-practice-type component. Thus a young medical student at Columbia, for example, sees the professor practicing privately at the Atchley Pavillion (the doctors' office building) adjacent to the hospital. They observe, albeit from a distance, that the professor is sharing an office, examining room, ancillary services in the building, and some services in the hospital. Rarely do they know anything about the specific pecuniary arrangements; however, they do see a role model who is seemingly carrying out a satisfactory private ambulatory and inpatient practice in a hospital-based setting.

A second and somewhat conservative explanation for this movement can be derived from an interpretation of a keystone traditional value of medicine described by Talcott Parsons as being a commitment to high technical competence.[7] Until a few decades ago, technical competence was primarily related to what doctors carried in their heads and black bags. However, that too, has changed. Now diagnosis and treatment often require expensive equipment and technical staff which is beyond the capital reach of most individuals and which is not used often enough by any one physician to be economically reasonable. Grouping around an institution allows one generally to practice the type of medicine he or she has been trained for, and to do it without compromising one's professional or financial integrity.

THE HOSPITAL AND AMBULATORY CARE

From the hospital's perspective, ambulatory care has meant two things: the emergency room (ER) and the outpatient department (OPD). From a social, political, and economic viewpoint, these areas have generated more than their share of adverse publicity and problems. A partial laundry list of ER and OPD headaches could include: patient waiting times, malpractice suits, patient authorization, clinical and nonclinical staffing, facility utilization, and cost and reimbursement for care. However, to balance the picture, one must also see the positive side of these organizational components, which include the following: provisions of an obviously needed community service, a training ground for physicians, and a source of inpatient admissions.

Certainly, exacerbating any or all of these problems is the uncertainty about the future that each institution faces. Among such uncertainties are the likely demand for services, budget approval, reimbursement formulas, and legal and technological changes that could affect care. Who, for example, forecasted the legalization of abortions and the subsequent demand for outpatient abortion services? Who foresaw the ER becoming a substitute for the family practitioner—and having foreseen that, what really could have been done? This section will address the three major organizational issues of staffing, the future, and role definition.

The major *staffing* issue faced by most institutions is that of increased demand for ambulatory-care services at the same time as available medical personnel to deliver the care are decreasing. The ER and OPD have been traditional training grounds for house staff and medical students. Indeed, in the past, a one-month compulsory rotation into the "pit" has almost been a common denominator of graduate education. This loss of house staff personnel from the ER and OPD has largely resulted from the elimination of the free-standing internship, the shortening length of most residency periods, the increased vulnerability of institutions to lawsuits, and the unionization and collective bargaining of house staff.

The Alexandria and Pontiac Plans, where physicians group themselves to provide coverage, offer two answers to the ER problem. In
isolated instances, group practices have developed to handle the OPD
situation. But, in most instances that were observed, the OPD
staffing, which was usually handled by *per diem* physicians, tended to
be unsatisfactory from all perspectives.

A second major issue is that of an uncertain *future*, further clouded
by such pieces of legislation as P.L. 93-641. Institutions, starting to
be confused, even oppressed, by planning, are thinking about ways in
which they can most successfully compete for dollars—which usually
means patients. To be successful in the marketplace, an institution
must have a stable of physicians who can be counted on to admit
patients. In order to capture these physicians and hence patients,
institutions are developing a variety of attractive options, including
geographic full-time positions, or what seems to be the most popular
item, a doctors' office building. The risks to administration of having
a critical mass of physicians more intimately involved in the institution are probably outweighed by the probability of financial
disaster if the institution cannot "catchmentize" a population. This
concern for capturing and holding a market partly explains the great
hospital interest in the Health Maintenance Organization. The HMO
clearly gives an institution a toehold on a certain population and
allows for clearer forecasting and eventual organizational vitality.

A final organizational concern is that of *role definition*. Just as all
of us as individuals periodically ask ourselves "Who am I?" or "What
do I really want to be when I grow up?", organizations must and are
doing the same thing.

Many hospitals really want to be tertiary care institutions that are
only treating patients with the most esoteric diseases. Fortunately,
those diseases are few and far between, and thus international
referral centers are forced to do both the esoteric and mundane work
of the medical world. Indeed, in most instances it is even necessary
to do primary care to have enough secondary care cases. But all of
this is quite confusing because one organizes an entity differently for
primary, secondary, and tertiary care. The net result is a good deal of
organizational stress when these various needs start competing with
one another.

CONCLUSION

Some final comment should be made about the key issues facing
those hospitals which have been considering the ambulatory care
options.

One problem area that has continually decreased in importance centers on the legal implications of hospital-based ambulatory care. The old concerns of "corporate medicine" have now been displaced by the problem of negotiating effective and efficient contracts between providers, consumers, and institutions.

Finance is perhaps the most significant area. Capital financing and certificate of need is one area of concern. Simply stated, how do you get the money to build or renovate space for a nonclinic-type ambulatory care organization? Some solutions have included condominium office buildings, lease-back arrangements, and a host of other real estate approaches. A second problem is that of potential cash flow; starting a program and hiring staff usually precede getting patients. Once patients arrive and dollars start coming in, the financial problems can be minimized, although, as noted in an earlier section, the political problems may begin. Specifically, once any relatively small and cohesive group of physicians controls a significant percentage of admissions to a hospital, they also have the potential for a significant amount of policy influence over that institution.

A final and crucial observation is related to the scope of services provided by the ambulatory care program. Most planning for such programs and the resultant physician staffing are haphazard. A number of hospitals have fallen into financial as well as professional difficulties through lack of planning. A rational planning model which begins with community needs and ends with recruiting staff must be followed. Approaching the problem the other way around leads to disaster.

New and changed ambulatory care programs have generated much controversy in the past, and probably will in the future. The nay-sayers always exist, and perhaps in their adversarial roles help the yea-sayers to focus more clearly on the realistic strengths and weaknesses of the program. Based on this writer's observations, the key elements of success seem to be a community demand for hospital-based ambulatory care that is not now being met by office-based practitioners, as well as some venture capital for a project, a critical mass of committed physicians, and the technical backup of a strong hospital administration to assist in the planning and implementation of a program.

NOTES

1. National Center for Health Statistics, "Preliminary Data from the National Ambulatory Medical Care Survey" (unpublished), p. 9.

2. National Center for Health Statistics, "Physician's Visits, Volume and Interval Since Last Visit, United States—1971." "Vital and Health Statistics." DHEW Pub. No. (HRA) 75-1524. (Washington, D.C.: Government Printing Office, March 1975), p. 28-30.

3. L.J. Taubenhaus, "The Non-Scheduled Patient in the Emergency Department and Walk-In Clinic," *Bulletin of the New York Academy of Medicine* 49, no. 5 (May 1973): 419-426.

4. M.C. Olendzki, "The Present Role of the Community Hospital in Primary Ambulatory Care," in Center for Community Health Systems, Columbia University, *Community Hospitals and the Challenge of Primary Care* (New York: Columbia University Press, 1975), p. 55-79. Other illustrations can be found in S.B. Goldsmith, "Organizing for Primary Care in Community Hospitals: Five Examples," in *Community Hospitals and the Challenge of Primary Care*, p. 81-103.

5. U.S. Department of Commerce, *Statistical Abstract of the U.S.* (Washington, D.C.: Government Printing Office, 1975), p. 37.

6. Olendzki, *op. cit.*, p. 65.

7. T. Parsons, *The Social System.* (New York: The Free Press, 1951), p. 428-479.

Chapter 7

Isaacson Foundation Hospital Medical Center

To the casual observer, such as a patient or visitor, the Isaacson Foundation Hospital Medical Center is one organization, a superficial unity emphasized by the common usage of a 25-year-old red brick facility. On further inspection, one finds a common medical record for ambulatory and inpatient care, one medical staff, and a host of other indicators of unity.

In reality, however, this center includes three separate and distinct organizations: the Isaacson Foundation for Medical Research and Training, the Isaacson Hospital, and the Isaacson Clinic.

Both the Isaacson Foundation and hospital have 501 C-3 tax status as nonprofit corporations, thus exempting them from federal, state and local taxes. The foundation is also eligible for certain funds only available to nonprofit institutions. The clinic, on the other hand, is a fee-for-service doctors' partnership run for profit.

The history of Isaacson is not significantly different from that of a number of other "mini-Mayos," such as the Geisinger Medical Center in Danville, Pennsylvania, or the Lovelace Bataan Medical Center in Albuquerque, New Mexico. Its founder was the late John Isaacson, a surgeon who trained during the 1930s at the world-famous Mayo Clinic in Rochester, Minnesota. After residency, Dr. Isaacson set up practice in Caroltown, and subsequently took in three partners. The group grew rapidly, and by 1950 it had 35 doctors, who on an average day had 100 patients in the community's three hospitals. Problems of admission priorities at the hospitals led the group into building its own 100-bed private facility. By 1955, two and a half years after it opened, the new hospital needed expansion, and at that time the doctors decided to make it both a nonprofit and a teaching institution affiliated with the local medical school. The foundation was set up in 1965 as a "money drop" for certain research and teaching activities.

In spite of its exurban location, the hospital and medical staff views itself as an international medical center. However, over 95 percent of the patients are within a 25-mile radius of the hospital, and almost all of the rest come from within the state. Nevertheless, the center's teaching programs are well respected, and there is rarely a shortage of qualified applicants for the 95 residencies and fellowships at Isaacson.

POLITICS AT ISAACSON

It is somewhat ironic that the Isaacson Hospital Medical Center is known as the bulwark of conservative medicine in the community. It was only several decades ago that Isaacson was considered somewhat radical because it had one of the state's first group practices. The physicians who joined this group were barred from all other staffs in the community and for several years were unable to join the county medical society. This ostracism passed with both time and two important changes which greatly helped to establish the legitimacy of the hospital and its doctors: the hospital becoming a nonprofit institution in 1955, and its affiliation with the local medical school several years later. At present the core of the county medical society comes from the Isaacson Clinic, and two past presidents of the state medical society were also clinic members. In local circles it is often said that the Isaacson Clinic doctors make more money and have more free time to devote to medical politics than the town's other private practitioners.

A different type of politics goes on within the Isaacson organization. When the center was founded, it was quite clear that the power group was made up of old-time surgeons and physicians who came to work with John Isaacson. Indeed, the surgical department was highly respected for its medical work, impressive generation of revenue, and probably the best-organized staff in the clinic. Internists basically were seen as ineffective "feeders for the surgeons."

With the passing of John Isaacson and two of his original group of senior surgeons, three new groups have come into controlling influence. These are the hospital's board of trustees, the senior administration, which includes the clinic's and hospital's administrator, and a group of physicians who could loosely be defined as the primary care doctors—internists and some general surgeons, as well as pediatricians and occasionally obstetricians, depending upon who defines the group.

The power base of this third group seems related both to their longevity at Isaacson and their involvement in teaching programs. However, there is considerable conflict between this group and the secondary and tertiary care specialists. The issues revolve less around money and more around the medical care direction of the hospital and the clinic. The fundamental question is whether the center should move more in the direction of a tertiary care organization or toward becoming a secondary care institution, with tertiary care capabilities and a defined primary care component.

ORGANIZATION AND MANAGEMENT

To talk of the organization and management of the Isaacson Hospital Medical Center, we must again recognize that we are dealing with three separate organizations: a hospital, a clinic, and a foundation.

The hospital is basically a traditional voluntary institution with a self-perpetuating board of trustees, consisting of seventeen individuals who include two physicians elected by the medical staff. The hospital's chief executive officer also sits as a board member and has the title of administrator. Half of the board are community people who are primarily the local elite, including bankers, attorneys, and businessmen. The other half are also prominent individuals proposed and elected by the foundation. Thus, it is obvious that the controlling power within the board and essentially the hospital is the Isaacson Foundation.

The clinic is quite differently organized. The top layer of its power structure consists of an executive committee of seven elected partners. The partners elect a medical director, who serves full time with a salary of $60,000. The medical director is the chief negotiator between the clinic, hospital and the foundation over space, rates for certain shared services, such as laboratory and x-ray, and other issues that develop. The other six members of the executive board essentially act as a policy advisory committee to the medical director. The present medical director has held that post for 14 years and sits as a voting member of the foundation board.

To carry out the clinic's traditional administrative functions, such as housekeeping, scheduling and staffing, the medical director has a clinic manager and two deputies. These clinic managers operate as business and personnel managers, and they neither sit on the executive committee nor on the foundation board. The senior clinic director has been with Isaacson for 22 years, and had previously been

the personnel director of the Brooks Corporation, a large manufac-
turer in the Caroltown community. He is well respected and
nationally active in the Medical Group Management Association,
where he was a past president. The deputy director has been at
Isaacson for seven years and is a graduate of the Columbia University graduate program in hospital administration. It is anticipated
that he will be leaving within the next six months to become
manager of a new clinic being developed in the southwest. The other
deputy director has been with the clinic for seven years and is
expected to replace the present clinic manager, who is retiring
within the next three years. He is a graduate of Tulane's graduate
program and has also been quite active in the affairs of the Medical
Group Management Association.

The third component of the Isaacson Hospital Medical Center is the
foundation. This is clearly the seat of power in the organization, and
also the most difficult part to understand. Both its anatomy and
history seem quite simple. The foundation was established as a
nonprofit corporation to raise money for Isaacson's research and
training programs. Subsequently, it became the owner of much of
the center's physical assets. Its board is made up of six people,
including the foundation's president. The board, through ownership
of the physicial facilities, control of certain funds, and its moral
leadership, derived from the board's composition, exerts the most
significant power in the medical center. No major decisions are made
or implemented without the express review and approval of the
foundation board.

MEDICAL CARE AT ISAACSON

The heart of Isaacson's system and what distinguishes it from
other institutions is its ambulatory care organization (the clinic),
with over 75 separate services. All medical care at the clinic is
provided by a partner, associate, or resident under the direct supervision of a partner or associate. The strictly enforced policy is that
private patients will be asked if they are willing to be examined
and/or treated by a resident; if acceptable, they are seen by both the
resident and "attending". Medicaid patients are also seen at the
clinic and are invariably residents' private patients; the supervision,
while existent, is not quite as obvious or intense.

The emergency room is a hospital responsibility and coverage is
provided by rotation of all first-year residents. At various times,
there has been talk of allowing a group of emergency room physicians

to set up practice at Isaacson, but this idea has not been viewed favorably by the medical staff. The emergency room is not particularly busy because of the proximity (two miles) of a large county hospital and the propensity of the county's volunteer ambulance squad to take patients to that facility. This is a situation which is viewed with favor by Isaacson staff; they do not consider, nor do they want, their emergency room to be an important source of patients.

The health maintenance organization (HMO) is the final element of the ambulatory care program at Isaacson. Although nonfunctioning, a considerable amount of foundation attention has been directed at planning an HMO; at this point, financial market feasibility studies have been completed. Although the medical staff has been extensively involved in these activities, there is a general apathy about the HMO and some negative talk regarding the amount of money that has been spent during the past three years on this program. When queried about the slow pace of the HMO development, it became obvious that it was a deliberate attempt to buy time while developing the expertise to deal with what appears to be an unpleasant, inevitable situation.

The leadership for the HMO planning comes from Dr. Benjamin Louis, a 37-year-old internist with training in public health and a career that has included Peace Corps and public health service work, but no private practice. Dr. Louis holds the title of Director of Community Medicine and is paid by both the foundation and the hospital. Well-liked by most medical staff, he is thought to be far too liberal in his views and is generally not supported on any significant program development, such as implementing a pilot HMO. He has, however, during his three years at Isaacson been able to inaugurate some less dramatic changes, such as an occupational health program, an executive health program, and a school health contract. Despite his setbacks, Dr. Louis remains "optimistic... if we're going to change the system, we're going to have to be successful in a great medical center like this, not just the city and county hospitals."

Inpatient care is provided at the hospital by the clinic staff and the 95-person house staff who are residents in 14 specialties (85 percent of the house staff are graduates of American medical schools). The teaching programs are organized in a traditional manner and are for the most part kept within the medical center, although several subspecialty training programs are jointly sponsored with a nearby medical school.

Nonmedical services are generally quite good at Isaacson, and, in keeping with its teaching, research and service activities, many departments have extramural programs. For example, the hospital's nursing service is a primary teaching affiliate of the Caroltown Community College's nursing program and the State University's baccalaureate program. There is a dietary internship at the hospital, and social work students can do a three-month affiliation at Isaacson. Hospital administration residencies are available in both the clinic and hospital.

THE FUTURE

The board, medical staff and administration are quite proud of the medical center—and probably justifiably so. The medical care offered there is thought by most observers to be excellent. The physician staff is well-qualified and numbers more than a score of clinical professors. While the clinical research emanating from Isaacson is hardly earthshaking, it is certainly respectable and voluminous.

It appears that the organization is well-established in the community and in a firm position to keep its share of the market. The future as viewed by the key staff is bright, and Isaacson is prepared.

COMMENT

The Isaacson Foundation Hospital Medical Center was a product of necessity. Like many similar organizations, it was born out of a need for doctors to take care of patients in a way they thought appropriate.

Although no formal planning process is integrated into Isaacson's organization, it has been successful because of the lack of any significant competition for its excellent and highly organized services. What is most interesting is how it has built an exceptionally well-qualified staff by offering them a practice environment that meets a variety of their professional and personal needs.

The criticism directed at Dr. Louis is a most interesting situation. The board and administration are using him as a tracer for new programs and allowing him to be their lightning rod. In some senses, this is an unbelievably calculating and callous way of treating a person—but Dr. Louis seems to enjoy and thrive on it. Perhaps this is how a place like Isaacson has to face what promises to be a decade of slow but certain growth.

Chapter 8

Hunterdon Medical Center

For more than 20 years, hospital administrators, trustees, medical staff, and health planners have journeyed to the town of Flemington in west central New Jersey to visit the 200-bed Hunterdon Medical Center. Their attention has been drawn to this institution, located in a semirural community of 75,000 people, not simply because it is a good hospital, but primarily because of the unique health system of 400-square-mile Hunterdon County.

The system consists of a hospital with 35 full-time salaried specialists, 18 residents in family practice, 2 primary care group practices, and 30 family practitioners located in private practice in the 26 municipalities throughout the county. The visitor to Hunterdon sees a closed system where hospital-based physicians serve as specialist consultants to the family practitioner, and family practitioners provide a range of ambulatory and inpatient services and handle almost half of all hospital admissions. In this system, the emergency room is not cluttered with nonurgent problems, patients apparently have access to family-centered comprehensive care, primary care is delivered in the community, and secondary and tertiary care are provided at the hospital. In short, this community is fully involved with its hospital.

Invariably, visitors to Hunterdon Medical Center ask one fundamental question: "How replicable is Hunterdon; that is, can the model of the Hunterdon Medical Center be reproduced elsewhere?" The fast answer is "No," the explanation being that "Hunterdon is unique, it was started in a medical vacuum, and its survival and growth depended on that vacuum. To attempt a transplant where there is not a confluence of community needs, lack of services, and a highly motivated staff would likely be unsuccessful." Despite this seemingly pessimistic appraisal of the replicability of Hunterdon, a study of its complex organization offers significant insights to those interested in hospital-based care. These insights relate to the nature and importance of leadership, community involvement, medical staff organization, and planning.

HISTORY OF HUNTERDON MEDICAL CENTER

In January, 1946, the proposal for a hospital in Hunterdon County was presented to the county's Board of Agriculture. The subject was discussed and debated for the next year, and finally the board asked Dr. E. H. L. Corwin of the New York Academy of Medicine to survey the county's health and hospital needs. Dr. Corwin's comprehensive study, delivered to the board in January, 1948, basically suggested that the country considered building a hospital, but:

> To sum up, if Hunterdon County were to build just another hospital, I would be lukewarm to the proposition, but if this hospital is projected in terms of a progressive institution with a university affiliation, a model of its kind, aimed to bring what is best in medicine to the residents of a rural area, and has associated with it an active, full-fledged health center and a good follow-through social service, I would be strongly for it. It should not be difficult for such an institution to secure a good-size endowment. The opportunity is here, and there is unquestionably enough pride and business enterprise in this community to bring this plan for a hospital and health center to successful consummation.

Successfully consummate they did! In March, 1948, incorporation papers were filed, and the Hunterdon Medical Center was launched. A subsequent report by Dr. Corwin in August, 1948, offered the philosophic underpinnings that have guided much of this institution's development:

> The hospital as envisioned by the incorporators is not to be a medical hotel or a nursing home, as many hospitals unfortunately are, nor is it to be patterned after the Mayo Clinic or the Lahey Clinic. It is to be a true community hospital which will provide adequate hospital care to the inhabitants of the county, a health protection service and a diagnostic service for the convenience of local physicians. Recognizing that the care of the sick in rural areas, and for

that matter in the cities, devolves upon the general practitioner, the Hunterdon Medical Center wishes to provide
the physicians in the county utmost opportunities for professional development now and in the future, thus making the
highest type of medical service possible.

In other words, it is the intention of the Hunterdon Medical
Center to give to the practitioners in the county a firsthand
opportunity to participate in the development of the proposed institution and to pave the way for others to continue
the work in the community as well-qualified practitioners,
abreast of the times not only through secondhand information but from active association with a first-class medical
institution.

Such an ultimate result is feasible if the hospital from its
very inception is dedicated to that ideal and is developing as
a teaching unit. It is important to realize that when the
hospital becomes, for the time being at least, a part of a
collaborative project of a progressive medical school, its
organization and its efficiency become the concern and
responsibility of the medical school. There are definite
practical advantages which accrue from a close association
with a university. [Therefore] the Trustees of the prospective medical center have entered into negotiations with the
authorities of the New York University-Bellevue Medical
Center, and a tentative plan of an alliance has been worked
out which would be to the advantage of the hospital and
would make it possible for the University Medical Center to
fulfill the obligation, recognized by it as well as by some
other universities, of extending its influence beyond the
teaching of undergraduate medical students. If the plan
succeeds, it will result not only in a first-class hospital for the
37,000 people of Hunterdon County, but in a training unit
which will set the highest standards for the young people
who work and study in it. As a result, the New York
University-Bellevue Medical Center, as well as other medical
training centers, may be encouraged to establish similar
associations elsewhere.

When questioned recently about the importance of this medical-
school affiliation for the intellectual health and welfare of the medical
center, the president of the Hunterdon Medical Center's Board of
Trustees, who has held this position since its founding, stated, "I

think the medical school affiliation in the early days was absolutely essential to us." The affiliation allowed the center, in his opinion, to attract a higher caliber of specialist physicians and insured those physicians continued contact with the "mainstream of medical care."

Funding was also a rather important (and, in some quarters, legendary) element in the development of Hunterdon. Of particular interest were the community's financial support of the hospital and the involvement of private foundations in January, 1949, when the project had a bank balance of $240. Eleven months and countless auctions, fairs, theater parties, meetings, and personal solicitations later, more than $900,000 in pledges had been secured from over 70 percent of the county's families—all this in a nonaffluent community without professional fund raisers.

Finally, one must consider the significance of seed money in the community's quest for medical care. When asked the importance of the several hundred thousand dollars received from the Commonwealth Fund and Kress Foundation in terms of the opening, survival, and success of the Hunterdon Medical Center, the board's president replied:

Absolutely essential. We had just the concept, the vaguest kind of concept, and opened our fund drive. We planned the hospital during the Korean War—until the time we started taking bids, prices soared. We cut almost a million dollars out of the building at the last minute and still the prices came in at about $900,000 more than we had money for.
We had promised the community that all the money we had raised would be held in escrow. The only money we spent was Trustees' money. If we couldn't get the job done, we'd give the money back. We had a community council then of about 125 people from all the communities that had been active in fund-raising. We called them together and said, "Look, if you go broke, the Commonwealth Fund agrees to give us $250,000 if the community will go in debt for $650,000."
So we called the people together and gave them three options:
1. Give the money back.
2. To forget the University, forget everything, forget Commonwealth and build a little hospital in the middle of Flemington.

3. Go for broke!
Nobody voted to give the money back. Two said, "The little
hospital." Everybody else said, "Go for broke!"
Had the people chosen otherwise we would have been dead at
that point.

On July 3, 1953, the Hunterdon Medical Center opened with 95
beds, 8 full-time physicians, and a staff of 55 employees. Twenty-two
years later, it is still the center of the county's health system and in
many respects is a reasonably accurate reflection of the dreams and
aspirations of its planners.

ORGANIZATIONAL ARRANGEMENTS

Since its inception, the basic structure of the 24-member board has
not changed, but the nature of the administrative organization
responsible to the board has evolved from that of a medical director
(physician) with a single administrator to that of a medical director
in the top slot with several specialized administrators at the next
level. These five assistant directors are responsible for medical
affairs, administration, finances, data processing, and nursing. Formal coordination of this six-member management team is handled at
a weekly meeting; informal coordination is carried out continuously.
The board's president, who has an office in the hospital, is involved
to an unusual extent in the functioning of the institution. This close
working relationship between hospital and board has clearly worked
at Hunterdon. But one wonders about the future, when the present
board leadership passes on. Will others be able to provide the same
time and dedication to the organization? If not, will the health and
welfare of the institution be jeopardized by that lack of external
leadership?
The present medical director is an orthopedist who still practices 25
percent of his time, serves as both chief executive and chief of staff,
and generally coordinates activities with the board. He sees the
future of institutional leadership as not necessarily coming from the
founding fathers or first wave of recruits, but perhaps instead from
outside the institution—from physicians in community medicine who
tend to be more interested in health care delivery than in the more
narrowly construed discipline of hospital administration.
Interviews with the assistant directors for administration, nursing, finance, and data processing suggest that the functions of these

people are not significantly different from their counterparts in other
community hospitals. The one executive position that clearly differs
is that of the assistant director for medical affairs. The functions of
this position include the traditional ones as well as those of a medical
group manager. For example, the present incumbent deals with
professional and nonprofessional staff recruiting, salary levels, and
staff evaluation. Most recently, he has developed new methods of
remuneration for the full-time staff.

Organization of Clinical Services

All physicians associated with Hunterdon Medical Center practice
on a fee-for-service basis, some as hospital-employed physicians and
others as community practitioners. Those who are hospital based and
physically located at the hospital come from the traditional medical
specialties, such as surgery, internal medicine, and opthalmology. In
addition to these specialists, the hospital employs two board-eligible
family practitioners who provide patient care and clinical teaching at
the Phillips Barber Health Center in Lambertville, 12 miles southwest
of Hunterdon. The 30 community physicians—all of whom are board-
certified or board-eligible family practitioners and 75 percent of
whom were trained at Hunterdon—have offices in a variety of
locations throughout the county and generally operate in an individ-
ualistic manner.

The structure of the hospital's active medical staff is an important
mechanism for linking the hospital physicians and the community
practitioners. Medical staff committees are composed of an equal
number of full-time hospital-based physicians and community practitioners. An obvious manifestation of both the sharing of responsibility for patients and the mutual respect that generally exists is the
observation that the family practitioners admit and care for approximately 50 percent of the hospital's patients. Furthermore, both
groups are involved in the family-practice residency program, which
has a total of 18 residents (six each in the first, second, and third
years). Perhaps most important, both groups seem to view each other
as integral to their own professional, financial, and, indeed, intellectual well-being.

The full-time staff is organized into a number of services corre-
sponding generally with those of any other community hospital.
These departments carry out the traditional administrative responsibilities; that is, they organize call schedules, plan for growth and

development of services, and insure the delivery of high-quality services. There is, however, one important difference—the director of services is the primary negotiator with the medical director for the salaries of the physicians on his service. This negotiation is directly concerned with the operations of the Professional Service Fund, which is the heart, and perhaps the most controversial aspect, of the financing system for full-time physicians.

The following excerpts from the memorandum of agreement (dated January, 1973), which was signed by the full-time staff, describe this fund:

Professional Service Fund

A. The Professional Service Fund shall consist of:
   1. All funds derived from patient fees and from other professional services rendered by members of the full-time staff with the exception of royalties.
   2. Funds accruing from a division between the Professional Service Fund and the regular operating account of the Medical Center of money received for combined professional-technical services. (In the case of laboratory and X-ray charges, 70 percent to go to operations, 30 percent to PSF. In the case of electrocardiography and electroencephalography, 50 percent each to operations and PSF.)
   3. Such other funds as may specifically be contributed, donated, or granted from time to time in support of education, research, health and other professional activities performed by members of the fulltime staff under the direction of the Medical Director, as authorized by the Board of Trustees.
B. The Professional Service Fund shall be expended by the Board of Trustees of Hunterdon Medical Center for the following purposes:
   1. Salaries of members of the fulltime staff.
   2. Reimbursement to the regular operating account of the Medical Center for the salaries of auxiliary personnel, overhead, administrative services, supplies, maintenance, *et cetera*, required by members of the fulltime staff in the performance of their duties. The amount of the reimbursement shall be determined by the Board of Trustees at the end of each fiscal year on the basis of a

cost study conducted by a competent firm of accountants, and after a conference between the Professional Affairs Committee of the Board of Trustees, and Finance Committee of the fulltime staff and the Medical Director. Decisions shall be based on the understanding that income from the professional services provided by members of the fulltime staff shall not be used to cover regular operating expenses of the hospital, nor shall ordinary hospital income be used to subsidize services rendered by members of the fulltime staff.

3. Retirement program, membership in professional associations, insurance, travel, *et cetera*, as enumerated below.

Since the hospital's inception, the method of paying the physicians has undergone two major changes; and, according to some observers, more are likely. Originally, all physicians received the same salary regardless of specialty or billings, with slight variations based on longevity. In 1965, an incentive plan was introduced that provided the physicians with bonuses based on productivity, teaching, and community service. This system, which had few mechanisms for controlling overhead and an inadequate mechanism for monitoring productivity, resulted in increased overhead charged to the Professional Services Fund.

The newest plan, which is presently in force, provides each department with a prospective budget. This involves a series of negotiations between the department (primarily its director) and the hospital (primarily the medical director) over the objectives, anticipated volumes and expenses, needed resources, and services of the department. These negotiations result in a contract-type agreement between the department and the hospital for services and salaries. The effectiveness of the new plan is yet to be evaluated, but the historical development of this, as well as the previous financial mechanism, demonstrate the need for an organization to respond in an individualized manner to the drives of professionals. Seemingly, the idea of one salary level for all was acceptable at the earlier stages of the Hunterdon Medical Center's development; but, as time passed, physicians simply became more interested in being remunerated in some relation to what they considered their outside earning capacity.

Central to the functioning of both the hospital and the system of health care in the county is the hospital's closed-specialist-staff policy. This policy, incorporated in the bylaws, grants active staff privileges only to physician specialists who are *hospital based*. An eminently well-trained and well-respected specialist or subspecialist actively practicing in the immediate environs of the Hunterdon Medical Center would not, under the present bylaws, be eligible to hospitalize his patients and remain as their attending physician at the hospital. In the past several years, a number of specialists have considered entering private practice in the community, but, learning of the regulations denying them admitting privileges at the hospital, they moved on.

In response to the question "Have there actually been any legal challenges to this closed-staff situation?" the president of the board stated:

> No, nobody has actually taken this to court. We have been threatened by court suit on four or five occasions, but they read our bylaws and they accept the fact that we say this has worked for Hunterdon, and challenge it if you will, this is our position. It has worked for Hunterdon and we think that we are entitled to keep it.

> And the people of Hunterdon have put many millions into this unit and this is what has been working for them, and we're not about to change it. And they back away somehow.

The assistant director for medical affairs added:

> Our legal defense is predicated on our ability to demonstrate that we are meeting the community's demand for care. For example, if a physician approaches us and announces his intention to practice ophthalmology in downtown Flemington on Main Street, we would say, "We have a closed staff, and we are meeting community need in your speciality; therefore, we do not need any additional physicians in your specialty." If, on the other hand, we fail to meet the community's need for service in that specialty, we could be vulnerable to a successful legal action to obtain admitting privileges.

Finally, of fundamental importance to the whole system is the relationship that exists between the full-time and community practitioners, which is one of mutual respect, mutual concern, and, indeed, admiration for one another's work. While this may be a result of the close relationship developed with the full-time staff during the community practitioners' training period (75 percent of the county's family practitioners are trained at Hunterdon), it is also no doubt related to the relatively clear delineation of professional authority and responsibility for patient care. In general, the family practitioners handle ambulatory and inpatient primary care, leaving ambulatory and inpatient secondary care for the hospital-based specialists.   However, there are family doctors who do manage patients on services that are traditionally considered secondary and tertiary in nature.   For example, a number of the family doctors admit coronary patients to the intensive care unit and manage them without a specialty consultation, yet the family doctor is not operating independently, for his patient is constantly surrounded by students, house staff, and full-time members.

Ambulatory Care Organization

Ambulatory care is provided in the family practitioners' offices throughout the county, the specialists' offices at the hospital, the hospital emergency room, the Riverfield Medical Group P.A. in Clinton, the Delaware Valley Family Health Center in Milford, and the Phillips Barber Family Health Center in Lambertville. The last center is operated by the hospital as a primary care facility and is staffed by hospital-employed family practitioners.

Under optimal conditions, each patient would have as his first line of contact a family practitioner who, in addition to providing primary care, would be responsible for coordinating secondary and tertiary care activities. A description of this mechanism in practice appeared in the November, 1968, issue of *Hospital Physician*, in which the case of a carpenter whose eye had been hit by a flying nail is discussed by a Hunterdon County family practitioner:

> As soon as I saw that the eye was severely damaged—more seriously than I could handle—I called Dr. J.W., one of the two ophthalmologists at the Medical Center. He said, "Send him in" and two hours later he called me back to say the nail had pierced the cornea and that the man would be hospitalized for three or four days. After this man is discharged, Dr. J.W. will follow him for his eye problem, and then send him back to me. I will bill the patient for an office visit and I will see him in the hospital because I feel a personal obligation to see that he's well cared for. But I won't bill for these visits. They're just courtesy calls.

With few exceptions, family practitioners are in solo practice and carry on in an independent manner, choosing their own location, billing their patients separately, keeping their own style of medical records, and arranging their own office hours, vacations, coverage, and patient load. In general, this seems to work well: several studies and personal observations indicate that most people have a sense of being tied into the system. A clear manifestation of the system's effectiveness is the low utilization of the Hunterdon Medical Center's emergency room for primary care (an estimated 15-30 percent of the patient visits).

A recent development in family practice is the hospital's sponsorship of primary care group practice in two separate ways. This sponsorship was necessitated by the fact that practitioners were simply not moving to Hunterdon County, where medical care was needed.

The first approach is that of the Phillips Barber Family Health Center. This strikingly attractive facility of 5,000 square feet, built by bequests from the Phillips Barber Foundation, provides primary health care to approximately 7,000 people, and serves as a model unit for the medical center's family practice residency program, as required by the American Medical Association's Council on Medical Education in its "Essentials of Approved Residencies." The facility is staffed by two full-time hospital-employed family practitioners and four full-time-equivalent residents. There are daily record reviews, a continual informal audit system, and a sophisticated system of tracking morbidity of ambulatory patients.

The center's prime mission is to provide good, family-centered, accessible primary care. Toward those ends, medical records are kept on a family basis; the center is open from 8:30 a.m. to 5:00 p.m., weekends, Monday and Thursday evenings, and Saturday mornings from 8:30 a.m. to 11:30 a.m.; and physicians are on call and make house calls. A relatively self-sufficient operation, the center conducts basic laboratory work-ups, is involved in community health education, and contracts with a nonprofit transportation service (Progress on Wheels) for patients unable to get there themselves. The gross billings of the Phillips Barber Center in 1973 were $200,000, and the operating loss was calculated at $34,000 (a figure equal to the amount budgeted for indirect Hunterdon Medical Center expenses, that is, computers and administration).

The second approach to sponsorship of primary care group practice taken by the Hunterdon Medical Center can be seen at the Riverfield Medical Group, P.A., in Clinton. Here two physicians have leased the hospital's practice building. The *quid pro quo* of this arrangement is that the medical group pays rent plus its own utilities, housekeeping, and staffing costs, and the practice serves as a teaching unit for the Hunterdon Medical Center's residency program in family practice. The hospital, for its part, built the $280,000 building on land it was given and maintains the facility. The rental fee is set at a low level to offset the teaching provided by the physicians. Primary care services, medical records, and auxiliary services are handled in Clinton similarly to those at the Phillips Barber Center, with one major difference—the Clinton physicians are family practitioners who are not hospital-employed.

The county's ambulatory care specialists are based at the Hunterdon Medical Center. Thirty-five full-time specialists provide a full range of services in the diagnostic center of the hospital, which is open eight hours a day, five days a week. Each specialty service organizes its own activities, such as appointment systems and coverage. Although no formal mechanisms exist to control patient volume, an informal mechanism operates through discouragement of self-referrals and the general lack of primary care capability at the hospital. In addition, the physicians are generally recruited to the staff for their specialty expertise, not for their general medical care abilities. Thus, a cardiologist would be expected to function mainly in his specialist capacity.

New patients arriving at the hospital for ambulatory care are not required to have their complete histories taken and to undergo physical examinations; nor are specialty- or subspecialty-referred patients required to have any type of standard examinations. It is thus not only possible but probable that, despite the system's closed nature, patients receive episodic and fragmented specialty care. Records are centralized, and inpatient and hospital-based ambulatory service records are stored together on opposite sides of the same folder. However, when medical records are reviewed, the audit focuses on the inpatient side.

How is quality maintained in ambulatory care? The answer is primarily related to the hospital's commitment to medical education. As a medical-school-affiliated teaching institution, the hospital considers all its patients teaching patients, and therefore provides them care—whether by a resident, specialist, or family practitioner—that is constantly under formal and informal review.

This overriding commitment also results in the recruitment and selection of well-trained and highly motivated physicians. Finally, there are a host of intra and extramural scientific and educational meetings with which professional staff are involved. For example, all full-time staff physicians are on the clinical faculty of Rutgers Medical School, where many of them spend a day each week. Locally, there are medical staff meetings on the second Tuesday of every month (including educational sessions) and regular scientific meetings every Saturday morning, but these are reported to be sparsely attended.

By almost any standard, the Hunterdon Medical Center is an eminently successful organization. Prior to its inception, the people in Hunterdon County had few health care resources. Today, they have a modern health system that provides a wide range of services in a high quality, comprehensive, accessible and available manner.

COMMENT

The Hunterdon Medical Center is obviously a fascinating organization with a number of important strengths, such as a defined and loyal consumer base that is an effectively enrolled population, well-trained and located practitioners, and an excellent local and national reputation.

Its weaknesses appear most related to low physician productivity, apparent conflict over doctors' incomes, and a lack of managerial leadership juxtaposed with strong one-man board leadership and some concern about the depth of board leadership.

Additionally, a number of external factors are impinging on Hunterdon, including new interstate highways and suburbanization that bring along with them individuals with different value systems and expectations for and from medical care providers.

Issues to be faced in this case include those of planning for new leadership, defining objectives, developing strategies to meet objectives, and, finally, maintaining a rational system in chaotic times.

REFERENCES

Barbara, A.J. and Hune, Andrew D., Jr. "Specialist Plus, Not Versus Family Physician; A Setting Conducive to Effective Postgraduate Education." *Postgraduate Medicine* 20, no. 3 (September, 1956): 305-309.

"Community Hospital of the Year." *Architectural Forum* 96 (January 1952): 126-129.

"Family Nursing Home Visits Have Doubled in Ten Years." *The Democrat* (local newspaper, Flemington, N.J.), May 9, 1974, p. 30.

Ferretti, Fred. "Ranks of General Practitioners Growing in the United States." *The New York Times*, May 24, 1972, p. 49.

Hunt, Andrew D., Jr. "An Experiment in Teamwork." *Child Study* 34, no. 1 (Winter, 1956-57): 10-14.

Hunt, Andrew D., Jr. and Trussell, Ray E. "They Let Parents Help in Children's Care." *Modern Hospital* 85 (September 1955): 89-91.

Katcher, Avrum D., Jr. "Parents Help Care for Their Children." *Hospitals* 35, no. 5 (March 1, 1961): 83-86.

Lincoln, John A. "The Development of a Satellite Family Health Center." *Medical Care* XII, no. 3 (March 1974): 260-265.

"A Medical Center Emerges from a Community Survey." *Hospitals* 29, no. 3 (March 1955): 76-81.

Pellegrino, Edmund D. "The Role of the Community Hospital in Continuing Education: The Hunterdon Experiment." *Journal of the American Medical Association* 164, no. 4 (May 25, 1956): 361-365.

———. "The Role of the Local Community in the Development of Health Services: The Hunterdon Experiment." *Industry and Tropical Health* IV, Harvard School of Public Health (1961): 53-64.

Somers, Anne R. "Toward a Rational Community Health System: The Hunterdon Model." *Hospital Progress*, April 1973, pp. 46-54.

"This is a New Kind of Community Medical Center." *Architectural Forum* 99 (December 1953): 130-135.

Trussell, Ray E. *The Hunterdon Medical Center: The Story of One Approach to Rural Medical Care.* (Cambridge, Massachusetts: Harvard University Press, 1956).

Tuck, Jay Nelson. "The Family Doctor: Can an Endangered Species Make a Comeback?" *New York Sunday News Magazine*, August 26, 1973, pp. 16-17, 20, 38.

Twenty Years of Community Medicine. A Hunterdon Medical Center Symposium. (Frenchtown, N.J.: Columbia Publishing Co., 1974).

Wescott, Lloyd B. "Capable Trustees: Product of Sound Organization." *Hospitals* 34, no. 13 (July 1, 1960): 51-53.

———. "Costs and Returns To the Hospital as a Corporate Entity." *Journal of the American Medical Association* 176, no. 12 (June 24, 1961): 986-988.

———. "Innovation in Medical Staff Organization." *The Hospital Medical Staff*, March, 1972, pp. 14-19.

Chapter 9

The Vantz Hospital's Medical Office Building

The idea of a medical office building first surfaced at the Vantz Hospital in 1949, when the hospital received a bequest of an 11-room frame house from the estate of Jonas La Vantz, the son of Jacque La Vantz, a wealthy New England merchant whose 1-million-dollar gift provided the original capital for the Vantz Hospital. The then board president (who is now dead) thought the house could be remodeled and rented to staff physicians at a slightly less than prevailing rate. The medical staff, upon hearing of this idea, unanimously objected to it and signed a letter that stated no member of the hospital's medical staff would rent an office in the proposed building. The staff also implied that it would be extraordinarily difficult for any new physician to practice in that community if he chose to house his office on hospital property.

The exact reasons for the physicians' strong negative reaction have been lost to history. Some of the older physicians have attributed the medical staff's reaction to a fear of an insidious version of socialized medicine—they thought the hospital would start to control their medical practice. One practitioner put it this way: "Greenville had a strong tradition of private practice. This office building was seen as an encroachment that would be the beginning and would not stop until all the doctors were hospital employees."

As a result of the physicians' stand, the building became the personnel offices for the hospital, and talk about doctors' offices at the hospital faded away for another 12 years. The second occasion for such discussion was precipitated by a decision to expand and modernize the hospital from its original 100 beds to 175 beds. As part of the planning for these capital expenditures, a joint board, medical staff and administration committee was put together to investigate the feasibility of either a doctors' office building or suites of doctors' offices at the hospital. The committee considered a number of issues including: the relationship between the doctors and their offices and the hospital, the probable patient reaction to such a set-up, the cost to the doctors and the hospital of offices, and the need for doctors' offices in the community. This committee recommended that neither a doctors' wing or a doctors' office building was needed—the demands for office space were being adequately met. At the time, the hospital's medical staff size was fairly stable, the community, although located 35 miles from a large city, had started to experience only moderate growth, and most of the staff simply could not foresee any need for change. Indeed, there was considerable conflict over the addition of 75 beds, since many of those involved with the hospital could not envision these beds ever being filled.

The third (and final) time discussions began about a medical office building was in 1975, after the medical staff passed a resolution asking the hospital's administration to investigate the feasibility of building such a facility. Much had changed in Greenville by that time. The population had doubled to almost 85,000, and the hospital now had 197 beds with a 71 percent occupancy, 585 employees, and a budget of slightly over 5 million dollars. In 1969, a new wing added 22 beds, as well as a series of upgraded services, including a radio-isotope diagnosis and treatment center, an intensive cardiac care unit, and a new emergency room.

All through this period of a growing physical facility and community one thing did happen—physicians were reluctant to settle in the Greenville community. Older physicians were retiring without replacement and younger physicians tended to be attracted to other exurban communities. For the practicing physicians this meant longer work hours, a heavier patient load, and cutting back on certain activities, such as hospital rounds, house calls, professional meetings and, in several instances, vacations.

One solution envisaged by the medical staff was that of a medical office building. They felt that this had been a successful solution at other hospitals and that attractive, well-located, and possibly cheaper space could be developed at the hospital.

A Board of Trustees subcommittee, with representatives of administration and the medical staff, was appointed to study the feasibility of a building. The major issues they addressed were the building's location, its ownership and governance, the organization and management of the building, and finally, the doctors' relationship to the hospital.

LOCATION

The first issue the committee addressed was whether the building should be on or off site. The arguments for an off-site location related to what was viewed as the present less-than-optimum location of the hospital. New housing tracts had been developed several miles south of the present hospital. Despite the relatively high cost of land, several committee members felt that for the convenience of doctors and patients the building might be in the south Greenville area. Arguing for an on-site location was the administrator and board chairman, who felt that the land would be cheaper; that the doctors would be closer to the hospital and its ancillary services, thus possibly eliminating the need for some facilities, such as x-ray or laboratory, in the building; that the nearby hospital would provide a backup cadre of physicians in case of disaster; and finally, since public transportation was virtually nonexistent in Greenville, the hospital location posed no special problems for patients.

The final decision was to place the building several hundred feet away from the hospital across from the main parking lot, which would be shared by both buildings. Some thought was given to having the building attached to the hospital. This idea was finally rejected, ostensibly because it would inhibit the expansion of both facilities, but perhaps more because, as one doctor noted, "It makes us look like we're working for the hospital and none of us want that."

The location established the independence of the medical office building, at least from an image perspective, although the initial building plans included a tunnel connection between the hospital and the doctors' offices. A later version of the plan, primarily dictated by a tightened capital budget, eliminated the tunnel and provided for a covered walkway. This, however, because of cost, was eliminated prior to construction.

A variety of options were considered by the planning group, including leaseback arrangements, private ownership, and finally the one that was selected, hospital ownership and control. This decision evolved from the hospital's reluctance to turn over its land to any type of private ownership and its desire to ensure that certain competing activities, such as ancillary services, did not develop in the medical office building.

Governance *per se* is not now an issue. However, during the initial planning of the building, it was anticipated but never articulated that the administrator would assign the space and act as the rental agent. Such an arrangement was unacceptable to the medical staff, who viewed it as an intolerable administrative power play. At present, each doctor individually signs his lease with one of the hospital's assistant administrators, who functions as the part-time building manager for support services such as housekeeping and maintenance. The individual management of each doctor's office is a personal matter, and thus specific office hours and staffing patterns vary. The only similarity is the modular physical design of the 900-square-feet suites, which were built to allow for rapid reconfiguration of interior spaces.

The specific decision as to who should be allowed to rent space is made by the hospital's space allocation committee, started in 1976 as a joint committee of the board and medical staff. This group reviews applications for space and decides on a doctor's suitability based on the criteria of specialty and the nature of the doctor's relationship with the hospital. For example, the committee recently declared a moratorium on internal medicine specialists in the building, and in several instances they refused space to doctors who had a primary affiliation at another hospital.

ORGANIZATION AND MANAGEMENT

The key problems of concern to all parties related to the following three issues: centralized vs. decentralized medical records, appointment systems, and billing systems.

In general, most doctors wanted to maintain their own medical records, but some agreed that a central system would likely benefit the patients in case of emergencies. However, it was also felt that a centralized system tended to "smack of a clinic," and a clinic environment was to be avoided at all costs. The result is a decentralized system in which all doctors maintain their own records as desired. The idea of using a standard problem-oriented-type record was also defeated.

The appointments system problem had two parts: the making of appointments and follow-ups, and the waiting room issue—i.e., should there be a general or separate waiting rooms? The area waiting rooms were not the medical staff's choice, but rather based on the need to cut back on space because of the escalation of construction costs.

The final problem related to the billing system. Everyone agreed that a central billing system would be most efficient. However, the reluctance of potentially sharing information about income led to the elimination of a business office function, although several doctors do have their billings done by a local bookkeeping firm.

The net result of these decisions is that each tenant has a similar and duplicative administrative/clinical set-up, usually consisting of a secretary-receptionist, bookkeeper, and one or two nurses. There is no pooling of staff or functions.

RELATIONSHIP BETWEEN MEDICAL OFFICE BUILDING AND HOSPITAL

The primary relationship between the MOB and the hospital is financial, with the hospital owning the space the doctors lease. Additionally, the hospital set up the requirement of staff membership in order to qualify for space in the building.

The actual physical linkages between the two facilities are minimal and limited to such things as electricity and heat.

There are obviously two different perspectives about this building. The doctors see it as a private building owned by the hospital, yet fairly well under their control in the same way that all tenants control their quarters. The hospital envisions the building as its "newest and most exciting" facility, part of the hospital, with the doctors there being the "nucleus of a geographic full-time staff." Indeed, the administrator foresees the time when some of the medical staff might even develop a "mini-HMO."

THE PRESENT AND FUTURE

As noted, there is some conflict and confusion concerning the present definition and future of the MOB. Since the opening of the building the trustees have generally maintained their distance. Administration has been actively involved in promoting the building and attempting to recruit physicians, partially by luring them with the attractiveness of the facility. The fears of the physicians about discrimination in terms of admitting, privileges, and administrative encroachment have not materialized.

The notion of some that the MOB should be a department of the hospital is an issue which is temporarily solved; that is, the MOB functions as virtually any other private medical arts building. However, the trustees and administration recognize that several things are occurring which may eventually move the MOB into something more hospital related. Specifically, some of the older physicians are now contemplating retirement; patients are starting to perceive the doctors as hospital based (this is an impression not based on any formal survey); there is some talk among the younger tenants of cross-coverage and joint administrative operations; and, finally, there are several preliminary (talking stage) proposals about a family-practice training program which may potentially involve the MOB doctors.

The bottom-line for the hospital is that its occupancy has increased slightly since the MOB opened, but no one is really willing to attribute that to the new building, except insofar as four new practitioners (one pediatrician, one internist and two family practitioners) have moved to town and into the building since it opened. No other practitioners have moved into the area. As a financial operation, the MOB has not been profitable; but it has not, despite the increased energy and operating cost, been a financial drain on the hospital.

On balance, most observers are pleased with the building and the decision in handling relationships. Some do suggest that the hospital has been far too generous with the staff, saying that physicians would have been recruited without the building, and that the building is another example of the hospital's unnecessary, nonpragmatic "edifice complex."

COMMENT

The popularity of the medical office building is perhaps best explained when one realizes that it is a conservative and incremental solution to many of the needs of the hospital, its medical staff, and the community.

To the hospital the building represents the possibility of a captured group of physicians and patients; to medical staff, a convenient practice arrangement which saves travel time and potentially has availability of high-quality ancillary services; and to the community it could represent a step in the direction of accessible comprehensive care.

The problems in any such development are delineated in this case, but the underlying issues that are still festering at the Vantz Hospital are related to the relationship of the medical office building to the overall objectives of the institution, and the strategy for the implementation of those objectives.

Part III
Hospital-Based Primary Care

Chapter 10

Hospital-Based Primary Care

The notion of hospital-based primary care services gives rise to two important conceptual problems: (a) what is meant by hospital-based, and (b) what is meant by primary care? However, even before addressing these important problems, a third question should be considered, which is, why should institutions be concerned about hospital-based primary care?

THE RATIONALE FOR CONCERN

Whether they like it or not, most institutions, as demonstrated in previous cases, are in the primary care business. The real issue is to what degree are they going to attempt to monitor, regulate, or utilize primary care to achieve their goals.

In many instances, the primary care is a result of external conditions. For example, in one hospital studied, the entire medical staff was composed of general practitioners because several years earlier a feud within the community caused many specialists in the town to resign from the hospital and take up practice in a neighboring community. Another external factor might be a state health or hospital code statute that requires an institution to operate an emergency room, but does nothing to regulate population usage of the facility.

Tradition is beginning to become another factor. As noted earlier, a highly mobile and to some extent disconnected population is developing its own traditions and pattern of usages—one of which appears to be, "when in doubt, turn to the local hospital for care."

Finally, the hospital, as almost any industrial concern, is forced into a horizontal integration mode in order to survive and prosper.

Thus, by offering primary care services that may be seen as competing with private practitioners, they are in some senses doing what is almost mandatory for the health of the organization and eventually the benefit of the private practitioners and their patients. Interestingly enough, this linkage and the delicate balance between the hospital, its competitive position, and the private practitioners' self-interest are rarely seen.

HOSPITAL-BASED: WHAT DOES IT MEAN?

Although the 7,000 hospitals in the U.S. would probably give that many different interpretations of the term "hospital-based," there would likely be several common denominators: physical, fiscal, organizational, and spiritual.

The *physical relationship* may mean that the primary care is being rendered within the hospital's walls or in buildings or land owned or leased by the hospital. In some cases, the services are delivered on the hospital campus, and in other instances they may be delivered many miles away. Three examples are illustrative of this point. At the Mountain View Hospital, the new clinic is located in a new doctors' office building that is owned, operated and physically adjacent to the hospital, while at the Hunterdon Medical Center we see several different approaches to off-site primary care operations, but all quite clearly hospital-linked. Finally, a third and perhaps futuristic type of hospital-based practice can be seen at Boston's Logan Airport. Here TV cameras and sophisticated telemetry equipment link a clinic at the airport with the Massachusetts General Hospital. Indeed, telemetry is found in mobile vehicles; they, too, use the hospital as a base station for their operations.

A *fiscal relationship* is in some senses both a clearer and more confusing relationship. Its clarity comes from what an accountant might describe as an "audit trail"—who gets what money for which purpose. The kind of financial relationship, however, can vary greatly. For example, a hospital may assume the total fiscal responsibility for a primary care program, as often occurs in teaching clinics; it may function as a "money drop" for government or foundation development funds; it may use its own capital or operating income to fund a program, or it may be the signer or cosigner of a note to finance a program; and finally, the hospital may operate as a real estate developer by leasing or renting space in some orderly and prearranged way to physicians who will practice certain primary care specialties.

An *organizational relationship* can be the most complex of all situations, ranging from subsidiary primary care groups to totally independent entities. Often within one hospital several organizational relationships for primary care might exist. For example, there may be a group practicing within the emergency room; an independent series of practitioners renting space in a doctors' office building, whose organizational relationship is that of tenant and medical staff member; an OPD which is treated as another hospital department; and a fledging HMO, which might be treated as an interdepartmental program with a staff, including physicians, who are hospital employees.

The last and most ambiguous relationship is labeled *spiritual*. This is when a hospital provides a modicum of advice and guidance to the primary care practitioners, but nothing more. The relationship from the practitioners' perspective is primarily warm and cordial, but also somewhat formal in that the practitioners' only official relationship to the hospital is that of medical staff. An interesting illustration of this spiritual relationship might be seen at the Hunterdon Medical Center, where the family practitioners are linked to the hospital by virtue of their staff privileges, alumni loyalty (approximately 75 percent of the family practitioners are trained at Hunterdon), and a referral system. The opposite side of the coin is the hospital's dependence on the family practitioners for referrals and approximately half of the admissions. However, the point to be stressed is that the relationship is generally that of caring for each other's general welfare, rather than one of formal organizational or financial ties.

PRIMARY CARE: WHAT DO WE MEAN?

Perhaps it is best to begin this section with a statement of prejudice: No open system is equitable, that is, inequities are an inevitable outcome of a system affected by any number of unidentifiable and uncontrollable variables. The best example is the primary school system in the U.S. Although there is indeed universally accessible and free primary education, the reality is that some schools are better than others, and some children have higher risks and opportunity costs to go to school than others. Further, primary education does not take place when children start school at ages five or six but rather from birth to the time they enter the educational system.

Focusing then on the health system, one could argue that medical practitioners have once again corrupted the English language in a self-serving manner by suggesting that primary care has something to do with a group of practitioners. Primary care is probably more related to individual health behaviors, such as smoking, drinking, weight control, seat-belt usage, and life style. When there is a need for corrective action, or advice and counsel, then a practitioner, perhaps a health educator instead of a physician, steps into the picture. Put simply, you cannot buy primary care.

However, common medical care usage has made primary care the first level of medical care. Since there is no general agreement on a definition for primary care, I will focus on those areas about which there appears to be a positive or negative consensus. First, there seems to be agreement in the literature and from practitioners that the medical specialties of family or general practice, pediatrics, and internal medicine are clearly primary care in nature, and that others such a neurosurgery, nephrology or opthalmology are not primary care specialties. However, two specialties are clearly in gray areas, surgery and obstetrics-gynecology. And after interviewing specialists in areas like urology and psychiatry, one realizes the difficulty of saying what is and what is not a primary care specialty.

Another way of approaching this question might be to say that all clinical specialties have within their practice some element of primary care. Specialties such as pediatrics or internal medicine tend to have the preponderance of their practice in the primary care mode, while specialties such as urology tend to have a considerably smaller primary care load.

Another area where some agreement seems to exist is that primary care services can be delivered by specialty-trained paraprofessionals, such as nurse practitioners or physicians' associates, under a physician's direction. In most instances, such care is envisioned as ambulatory and not inpatient, and the problems presented readily lend themselves to solutions.

Disagreement is primarily related, as noted earlier, to who should do it; who does it best (have you ever heard a debate between a board-certified family practitioner and a board-certified internist?); and of what value the care is for the patient. Finally, there is considerable debate over the boundaries of primary care—does it include social-service-type activities or what?

Regardless of such debate, the implications of primary care for a hospital are significant. The hospital's emergency room has been a focus for primary care; that is, patients who emerge from their own self-help systems enter the next level through the emergency room. Attempts to change this sort of patient behavior have been unsuccessful, and the hospitals continue to keep one of the most expensive areas of the institution on stand-by for the infrequent emergency.

Why do they do this? Let me suggest two reasons. First, the emergency room represents an important area of potentially positive (also negative) marketing for the hospital; and secondly, it is a source of patients for the inpatient services. Together, these reasons suggest that it would indeed be unwise to disrupt the flow of primary care patients to the hospital.

And for the individual practitioners, primary care represents "bread and butter" medicine and/or a source of patients for a referral practice.

For a hospital to put together a system with primary, secondary, and tertiary care components is eminently sensible. The hospital thus positions itself within a marketplace whereby it can forecast, plan, and control the bed utilization , and effectively offer a group of practitioners, through an established referral network, a guaranteed annual income.

Although the patterns of hospital-based primary care seem to be limited only by the number of hospitals, two have been selected for cases in this volume. Each of these represents different methods and processes, and similar problems and outcomes. Hopefully, they represent an opportunity to study the costs and benefits of the various approaches to hospital-based primary care.

Chapter 11

The Mountain View Hospital Clinic

In the spring of 1975, visitors from the Joint Commission on Accreditation informally reported to the Director of the Mountain View Hospital that the outpatient services and facilities available at that hospital were a "disgrace" and far inferior to what was available throughout the rest of the hospital.

By February, 1976, the outpatient department had been closed and a new organization, the Mountain View Clinic, was opened. The clinic was a fee-for-service, hospital-based, primary care group practice planned to deliver a range of inpatient and outpatient services in a cost-effective way to the old clinic population and a new population of individuals who were using the hospital's emergency room and other facilities for primary care.

BACKGROUND

The Mountain View Hospital is located in one of Michigan's industrial cities with a population now reaching 250,000. For many years, the industries and unions have encouraged and nurtured a health planning group, an activist medical school, and teaching hospitals.

The Mountain View Hospital is a 311-bed university type teaching hospital affiliated with the State University College of Medicine. This hospital, which had a 1973 budget in excess of $15 million dollars, 1,100 staff, and an average occupancy of 86 percent, is located in a low middle-class workers' neighborhood.

The Mountain View Hospital's medical staff was a patient-oriented group concerned about dual standards of care, the unavailability of primary care, and a poor physical facility in the outpatient department. Despite this concern however, there was no unanimity of opinion about developing an innovative ambulatory care program. Indeed, one veteran, recalling those days, noted that everyone heard about the program officially and had a chance to articulate their preferences to the trustees, senior medical staff, and administration:

> The coffee tables were click-clacking all the while. . . . But there was enough support for it so those people who were basically not in favor of this [reorganization] were really kind of outvoted. Although, . . . they were outvoted by quite a respectable margin—there is no way you are going to get 200 staff physicians to vote in unison on anything.

ORGANIZATION AND MANAGEMENT

The Mountain View Clinic represents a departure from the traditional hospital outpatient department mode of primary care because it deemphasizes pigeonholing patients into fragmented clinics, and its organization is strikingly similar to that of a traditional private group practice. This particular organizational design was developed in order to meet three objectives: (1) to offer mainstream medical care to traditional outpatient clinic users, (2) to encourage the clinic's use by middle-class patients, and (3) to gain the support, but noninterference, of the hospital.

The desire to offer mainstream medical care appears to have resulted largely from a sincere concern by the director of ambulatory care to give indigents the opportunity to receive the same medical care as private patients in a traditional group practice. A manifestation of this attitude is the policy that untried innovations in health care delivery should not be offered to indigents in the new clinic. Early in its design, Mountain View recognized that the middle-class population would more likely find traditionally organized group practices more attractive than a clinic. Consequently, Mountain View operates in well-appointed facilities (with a main waiting room that faces the Forsyth Mountains), is staffed by employees hired by the physicians, and each specialty area maintains its own decentralized receptionist and appointment-making activities.

The group's initiators were concerned from the outset with avoiding the development of poverty-program-type setup that would result in high physician turnover. They hypothesized that this could be best avoided by caring for a socio-economically balanced patient population composed of middle-class patients as well as traditional OPD users.

The concern with maintaining a balanced population has been so great that there is serious thought now being given to developing several "off-campus" ambulatory care centers in the middle-class suburbs.

Mountain View has also directed much attention to the maintenance of favorable working conditions for the physicians. Consequently, the physicians are offered many of the benefits of independent private practice, including physician control over the remuneration of the medical staff, over the hiring and firing of personnel, and the decentralization of a number of practice functions, including receiving patients and appointment making. Moreover, this independence also allows a high degree of self-governance. Physicians in the group are accountable to their own medical director, who is organizationally responsible to the hospital's vice president for medical affairs. Within the group, some physicians are designated as partners and others as associates; the partners are reimbursed on an incentive remuneration system based in large measure upon billings and the associates are salaried.

The hospital's hands-off attitude toward the group has reinforced the group's independence and high degree of self-governance. For example, the Mountain View physicians are free to associate with their parent hospital or not, depending on their own interests—although at present only two physicians hold appointments elsewhere, and it is rare for either to hospitalize their patients at the other hospital. Additionally, an advisory board made up of representatives from the hospital trustees, medical staff, and the community act as a consultative group on such matters as program development, staffing, and future directions for the clinic.

At present, the Mountain View Clinic is open 5½ days per week, 9½ hours, Monday through Friday, and 4 hours on Saturday. To staff the program, 46 people are required. The specific breakdown is:

Physicians

Pediatricians	3
Internists	8
Obstetrician-Gynecologists	2(FTE)
Pediatric neurologists	(on call)
Pediatric cardiologists	(on call)
Orthopedic surgeons	(on call)

Physician's Associate

    Internal Medicine   1

Nurses

    Registered nurses   3
    Licensed practical nurses   7
    Health assistants   1
    Pediatric nurse practitioners   1

Administration

    Administrator   1
    Bookkeeper   1
    Receptionists   2
    Accounts receivable clerks   2
    Medical secretaries   7
    Medical record technicians   3
    Medical record transport clerk   1
    File clerk   1

Maintenance

    Building and
      Grounds   Shared with hospital
    Janitorial   Shared with hospital
    Cafeteria   Shared with hospital

This staff handles an annual load of approximately 50,000 visits. At present, specific utilization data are unavailable but are being developed.

FINANCIAL MANAGEMENT

The total cost of the facility's renovation and provision of equipment and furnishings was $340,000. The sources of funds for the equipping and renovation came from several donations (including two sizable ones that equalled over $150,000) and loans from a local bank and insurance company.

The space utilized is owned by the hospital and rented to the group at what the medical director and hospital administrator describe as a fair market price, which includes the range of indirect allocated costs.

Within the practice, considerable effort has been expended to keep up a high collection rate. Thus, billing and initial collection attempts are handled from the M.V. business office, and the present collection rate is 83 percent compared with a 41 percent collection rate in the old OPD.

STRATEGY FOR CHANGE

Two elements crucial for change have already been identified and discussed in earlier sections: attitudes of the hospital staff, and the progressive nature of the community within which Mountain View finds itself.

Two other elements are worthy of note because of their obvious importance: money and leadership.

Certain funds came to the clinic for space renovation, furniture and equipment. This capital financing, while significant, may not have been as important as the hospital's willingness to absorb a deficit in the new clinic equal to the deficit of the old outpatient clinic. The stage was therefore set to give the new group something of a chance at success—it did not have to begin with an expectation of immediate financial solvency. Reimbursement for Medicaid services was linked to the hospital's rates, resulting in Mountain View having an office reimbursement somewhat higher than that of nonhospital-based private practitioners.

Leadership, however, does represent a particularly important success element. Regarding Mountain View, several people come to mind: the hospital director (president) who helped nurture a congenial environment for the program's development; the vice president for medical affairs, who informally led the medical staff away from the OPD towards the Mountain View Clinic; the medical director, who brought both a small private practice and a vision into the group at the very beginning of its life; and the group's administrator, who worked with the community and the hospital developing the management systems to ensure the group's viability.

A MODEL SYSTEM?

Is Mountain View replicable? Could a similar system of delivering health care services elsewhere be implemented, assuming there were start-up funds, the right organizational leadership, and a favorable financial environment (e.g., Medicaid reimbursement rates and relatively small population of medically indigent)? Yes, indeed, it would be possible, and in some sense this has occurred at other institutions. But there were costs attached to developing the Mountain View-type program, the most significant being the teaching program.

Prior to the new clinic's inception, an outpatient department existed which had as one of its primary functions the teaching of house staff. Indeed, no patient was accepted into the clinic unless he/she was an "interesting teaching case." For both philosophical and financial reasons, house staff teaching is nonexistent within the new clinic. This has resulted in the still embryonic development of various small specialty clinics around the hospital, which provide an opportunity for house staff to follow up patients on an outpatient basis. Another interesting development is that the hospital's department of medicine, in conjunction with the state university, has recently begun a training program in primary care internal medicine, which utilizes a suburban, private, multispecialty group practice as its principal ambulatory care teaching site.

If the Mountain View Clinic decided to provide an active teaching program, it would have to assume a major financial burden that would seriously jeopardize its solvency because of lost physician productivity, as well as direct costs. On the philosophical side, the clinic would risk the loss of patients, particularly private ones, who would not be interested in going to a classical OPD.

Despite the lack of a teaching program, the quality of care available to patients is of considerable group interest. At present, no formal system of peer review goes on, such as periodic chart audit. Instead, quality is maintained through the traditional methods of careful physician selection and such informal mechanisms as peer review resulting from cross-coverage and patient referral. These systems are recognized as only marginally acceptable, but the patient-demand pressures are such that to devote more time to a formal review program is not considered feasible.

Perhaps a different bottom-line question one must ask is whether the Mountain View Clinic could survive if cut loose from the hospital. Indeed it could! It is clear that the clinic's small hospital subsidy will not be required indefinitely as its cash flow continues to improve; these funds have served as risk reducers or venture capital, and not as operating subsidies. Therefore, despite the genesis of Mountain View as a hospital-based program, it appears to be evolving into a highly independent medical group that is organized similarly to that of a private group practice.

Finally, one must consider the perception of others about such a group. The building that houses Mountain View is also used by numerous other physicians on the hospital staff (some solo, others grouped). In general, they view the clinic with benign neglect, although some are quite approving of the physicians in the practice, while others simply ignore its existence. An almost universal opinion among the hospital staff is that the clinic is a dramatic and significant improvement over the old outpatient department. Further, even those physicians who were initially negative about Mountain View have changed their opinions and now refer patients to this group.

Initial medical staff scepticism toward the clinic was based on a variety of factors, such as a distrust of the group's leadership; a concern that Mountain View physicians were not going to pull their own weight (that is, they were going to be 9-to-5 doctors, abandon their patients to the emergency room, and not take their attending turns); and, finally, a confusion over what was being planned. A year later, Mountain View is thought of as a good investment; the physicians and administration have proven themselves; and, in general, the medical staff would not like to see a return to the previous system.

A limited number of patients interviewed during this case study provided a different perspective. To them Mountain View was an attractive clinic or doctors' office—it did not seem to matter which —where they found good care at a reasonable price and where the waiting was not too long. The fact that it was a primary care group practice with a single chart, which offered the potential for family-centered, comprehensive and coordinated care, did not seem to be of great concern to those interviewed. Overall, patients were pleased with the service, intended to return, and felt no hesitation to recommend the clinic to friends or family.

Administrators of other hospitals, as well as a variety of other health-concerned individuals not associated with Mountain View, generally presented a somewhat disinterested attitude toward the clinic. Indeed, some suggested that the only difference between their own ambulatory care operation and the Mountain View Clinic was a "PR machine." The program is not without its rough edges; but after two years, good physicians are delivering quality care in somewhat coordinated fashion, and the whole package is financially sound.

COMMENT

One wonders how rapidly Mountain View would have moved without the criticism it received from the joint commission and the financial support provided by benefactors. Regardless of these factors, however, it is an interesting example of a unique solution that has produced considerable benefits for all par.ies.

However, Mountain View is a program still in its infancy; and despite its successful traversing of the neonatal phase, one must consider the next phases of growth and development.

The environment is no longer hostile, but who should take the lead in making the environment actively supportive? Who should set the expectations for the program, and how and where should rewards (and perhaps punishment) be delivered?

The next two or three years are crucial for the Mountain View Hospital Clinic's continuing success. The question remains, can the same type of leadership already demonstrated maintain that success?

Chapter 12

The Mercy Hospital Emergency Group

The Mercy Hospital in Libertyville is a fully accredited, 300-bed, nonprofit voluntary hospital serving an eight-mile geographic radius that encompasses 11 towns in the northwest part of the state with a population of approximately 150,000. The industrial base of Libertyville is somewhat limited: there are three medium-sized plants (remnants of a predepression boom) and several hotels serving the community, which is also an "almost ran" skiing area in the winter and a locally popular hiking area in the summer. In 1975, the hospital's 13,000 admissions resulted in an 81 percent overall occupancy rate, with medical and surgical occupancy in excess of 95 percent. The institution has a 200-person medical staff, 1,000 employees, and an annual operating budget of 20-million dollars.

Ultimate control of Mercy Hospital rests with a 28-member board of directors and a 7-member executive committee. Community involvement is seemingly substantial through a wide variety of mechanisms, including an active junior board, woman's auxiliary, and various community liaison activities. There is a consensus among the staff that the power within the organization tends to reside with a small, select group of trustees and the hospital's president.

Reporting directly to the president are a variety of associates, including the full-time director of Mercy Hospital Emergency Group. The group is responsible for emergency services, as well as follow-up on patients seen in the ER who do not have, or have elected not to see, their own primary care physicians. Coordinating and monitoring the ER's operations is a committee of attending medical staff. One observer described the history and functions of this supervising committee as follows:

This all goes back nine years when the hospital first got into this full-time coverage of emergency room service. There was strong concern on the part of the medical staff that the hospital not enter into the private practice of medicine. In their view, although it was the medical staff committee that recommended this organization, there was still a lot of concern on their part that this would be a real invasion and foot in the door, and all that kind of thing. So rather than give the director of the emergency room equal status with other chiefs of service, they layered-in this emergency room committee.

As far as the medical staff is concerned, it's the committee which is the watchdog of the emergency room, monitoring the quality of care, and making sure that it doesn't become a full private practice of medicine.

DEVELOPMENT OF THE EMERGENCY ROOM GROUP

In 1970, a general practitioner and active Mercy Hospital practitioner agreed to retire from private practice and assume responsibility for organizing a group of physicians to deliver medical care in the emergency room. The conditions he and, subsequently, his group agreed to were no patient follow-up (except to remove or check sutures and casts) and no admitting privileges in the hospital.

By 1974, the medical staff recognized the difficulties experienced by patients in obtaining follow-up care, and a primary care center was introduced as a part of the emergency room. Also, the emergency room was divided into two separate areas, trauma and nontrauma.

The director explained how the medical staff reacted to this:

There was reluctance on the part of the medical community to approve the idea of partitioned care because they saw the hospital going more and more into the practice of medicine. However, we indicated to them that if any of the doctors wanted new patients, they should just let us know and we would see that they are referred to them.

That offer quieted them down a little and most doctors are *not* taking new patients.

We began to refer specialized cases out to the specialists and have established quite a good rapport.

Now we are giving follow-up care for those people who can't

get a private physician to look after them...and now that is amounting to only about 180 cases a month in continuing care.

FISCAL CONSIDERATIONS

In 1975, the budget for the emergency room was $873,000, and its income amounted to $810,000. Included in this were the usual direct expense items, such as salaries and supplies ($583,000), as well as indirect costs resulting from the expensive and relatively new facility housing the emergency room.

Patients using the emergency room are billed $17 for the service (the hospital collects $15.36 from Medicaid). If a private practitioner uses the emergency room to see his own patient (as happens with 13 percent of the patients coming into the ER), the patient is billed $10 for the use of the facility in addition to the doctor's fee, which is billed separately.

Income to the Emergency Room comes from:

Medicare	4.4%
Blue Cross	32.1%
State welfare	6.7%
Miscellaneous (private payment and commercial carriers)	55.5%

Uncollectibles are 26 percent of the 55.5 percent miscellaneous figure, or an overall rate of 14 percent. Additional income for the hospital is generated by the group's 10 to 12 daily admissions to the hospital, and approximately $900,000 comes from yearly charges for laboratory, x-ray and other ancillary services.

PATIENT FLOW

Trauma patients (representing 6-8 percent of the case load) come in via police, ambulance, or private vehicles and are directed into one of the three trauma rooms. These rooms, fitted with excellent equipment, can service a total of nine patients.

Communication between vehicles in the field and the hospital is somewhat limited at present, with the Fire Department having the only direct radio contact with the ER. All others, including the police, must relay calls.

Nontrauma patients enter through a well-marked emergency entrance, where they are met by white-uniformed clerk-secretaries who perform both the triage and data-gathering functions. After initial screening and the completion of forms, the patient is seated in a small waiting area. Questions routinely asked during intake procedures include: Why are you here? Have you ever been here before? Do you have a private physician? Shall we call your private physician?

Prior to a nontrauma patient's visit, files are searched for records of the patient's previous visits, and these are given to the attending physician. Patients are billed by the hospital, but if they wish to pay in cash, it is collected by the receptionist in the ER group on a voluntary basis.

A radiological examination involves a short trip down a corridor, while laboratory work generally requires that a lab technician come into the ER.

Patients interviewed in the ER were waiting to be seen for a variety of reasons, ranging from minor accidents to general medical care and depression. Perhaps because Libertyville is a fairly small community, many patients had private physicians who were just too busy to see them immediately; they were using the ER because "Once we get here, we know we'll be seen." None of those interviewed had a sense that they were in anything other than a traditional ER; they were not aware of the continuing-care program or the hospital-based medical staff.

PERSONNEL

Nine full-time physicians and a number of part-time "moonlighting" residents from University Hospital staff the ER. Full-time physicians include the director (who spends half his time administering the program), one board-certified internist, three general practitioners, two recently trained foreign surgeons, one physician with a specialty in nuclear medicine, and one surgeon. The surgeons work a 37.5-hour week, with limited educational leave time (once every four years a surgeon will be sent to an emergency-medicine course), four weeks of annual vacation, and the usual range of hospital fringe benefits. Salaries for these positions start at $45,000. Physicians on eight-hour shifts are paid between $200 and $225 per tour. None of the physicians have admitting privileges to the hospital.

In 1976, the ER group staff totaled 29.7 full-time equivalents; in addition to physicians, this included one physician's assistant, 8.6 nurses, and 6.2 clerical personnel. A typical shift consists of two physicians, three nurses (one in the trauma area, one in the non-trauma area, and one in the doctors' private patient area), 1.5 aides, two secretaries, one clerk, and several volunteers. The nurses report to a nursing supervisor, who is responsible to the group's director. Secretaries and clerks report to a hospital department supervisor.

Operational problems identified by the staff were primarily focused around the heavy utilization of the facility by private practitioners and the dual lines of authority and responsibility.

Recruiting of physicians is handled by the department with the approval of the primary care committee and administration. Basically, it is up to the group and its director to hire and fire appropriately-qualified physicians for these jobs. A variety of informal mechanisms are utilized in recruitment; for example, the three physicians employed most recently were previously moonlighters at the institution. However, despite the availability of people to fill ER positions, no particular effort has been made to balance the group with different specialties.

In general, no other staffing problems were identified, and the only innovation noted was the ER's employment of one physician's assistant and one student-physician's assistant. The physician's assistant performs a full range of services, including suturing and casting; and despite some early resistance to his hiring, he is now well-accepted, indeed praised, by the staff.

RESEARCH, STATISTICS AND EVALUATION

ER reports are kept in the hospital's central file, which holds a unit record for each patient. Additional copies of the record are sent to the patient and the patient's private physician, and one copy is filed for six to eight months in an ER record room that is staffed 16 hours per day. These files are checked when a patient arrives for a visit, and the available records are given to the attending physician before the patient is seen.

Quality-of-care evaluation is somewhat limited. In the past, some chart review was performed, but the pressure of 200 visits per day precludes any such review at this time. In a recent effort to maintain quality, each physician will spend one hour a week with a cardiologist reviewing EKGs and related problems. Although the group has suggested areas in which continuing education would be valuable, mechanisms have not yet been developed to provide that education.

The quality-of-care issue seems to be an area of some concern. From the board's perspective, care is quite good. Some practitioners share this view, even to the point of "signing out" to the ER. Others think the quality of care is of a lower level than that available in their own private offices. The few patients who fill out the opinion questionnaire available to them in the waiting area are generally pleased, although they mention a number of nonquality-related problems. In general, though, it was agreed to by all that, despite a variety of shortcomings, ER care at Mercy was significantly better now than before the group took over.

GROUPING IN THE ER

Medical care purists may object to the liberal use of the term "group" throughout this case study. After all, they may argue, "These people don't really share—they don't pool income, share expenses, or cross-cover, and they use the hospital's facilities—so how are they a group?" The purists' statements are indeed correct. But let us reconsider the American Medical Association's definition of group practice and evaluate this group accordingly:

> Group medical practice is the application of medical services by three or more fulltime physicians formally organized to provide medical care consultation, diagnosis and/or treatment through the joint use of equipment and personnel, and with the income from medical practice distributed in accordance with methods previously determined by the members of the group.

What we find at Mercy are nine physicians from three specialties (general practice, internal medicine, and surgery), providing a wide spectrum of medical care to patients from a poorly defined population. These physicians jointly use equipment and personnel, and have their income in some measure determined by the group (in the sense that the group's income is related to the revenue produced by the group, although no exact formula exists). Furthermore, we do see a certain commonality of concern: "How do we handle patients walking into our area?" "How do we gear ourselves for the winter onslaught?" "Should we continue to participate in the house-staff teaching program?" And we also see some attempts at functioning like an organization (e.g., monthly staff meetings).

What is not observed is a commitment to group practice, as well as a commitment, or even an opportunity, to deliver continuous care to a population. For example, in many respects the ER physicians see themselves as adjuncts to the private practitioners. They do not, nor do they intend to, compete for patients with the private practitioners. Indeed, one can surmise that by providing episodic care, the physicians feel they are filling an important gap in availability of health services while leaving the responsibility of continuity to others.

The commitment to the group is perhaps a double-edged sword, raising the question of how committed the hospital is to the group. Physicians joining the group have no direct pecuniary interest in the operations such as one sees among partners in a fee-for-service group practice; nor does the hospital grant them tenure. In many ways, the group functions as a way station for some people and a good retirment position for others. Is that commitment?

Sharing of information on patients among group physicians is minimal, and occasionally a problem of some concern. More significantly, the sharing of medical experience on a peer-teaching basis was not in evidence. While this should be one of the major group practice benefits to the physicians—and, indirectly, to the patients—the possibility of informal teaching is almost negligible because of the heel-in-toe schedule, which leaves no more than five physicians together for more than a short period of time.

Concern over these problems has led to the aforementioned thinking on continuing education, the decision to have monthly staff meetings, and discussions about mechanisms for more effective communication.

FUTURE DIRECTIONS

It is probably fair to say that many people, while satisfied with much of the progress in ambulatory care at Mercy Hospital, believe that much still remains to be done. Furthermore, a number of newly developing situations (e.g., a new medical school affiliation) are likely to affect the organization and delivery of ambulatory services at the hospital significantly.

A central question one might ask is, "To what extent is delivery of primary and ambulatory care likely to be the hospital's future role?" At this point, it is clear that the institution is reluctant to alienate the staff's private practitioners. It is also evident that these private physicians are both committed to the hospital and an unactuated power bloc. Evidence of such commitment is dramatic: for example, in 1963, 12 physicians had their offices near the hospital; in 1976, 26 were so located. These physicians, while agreeing that there are more than enough patients for every practitioner, fear the hospital's competition, which could be in the form of a doctors' office building or a real group practice that is hospital-based.

What is this fear about? It is certainly not a concern for losing patients. Rather, it is a concern about losing beds. The scenario, as described by one leading private practitioner, would first involve something innocuous like the office building, later a priority system on ancillary services, and finally a priority for the "hospital doctors" regarding beds. From the hospital's perspective, this is unrealistic, but to the practitioners this situation already exists. For example, complaints are heard about delayed laboratory or radiological examinations because the ER is tying up the service.

Will the ER group be the base of some future hospital-based primary care group practice or HMO? Some people, both in and out of the hospital, think and hope that it will. The director is not one of the supporters of such a development. His interest is basically in serving walk-in patients and turning them back to the private practitioners.

Others in the group have talked of the possibility of an HMO, but the viability of such a development must be questioned when the HMO concept and its implications are obviously poorly understood, and the practice environment is such that physicians "sign out" to the emergency room. As one group member observed:

> Because they know they will get the patients back, they know they can always get a record of what happens to the patient here; they know that if there's something—if the patient needs any other specialty services outside of their area, the fastest way to get them—much faster than going through the physician's appointment service—the fastest way to get the other specialty services to come is through the emergency room. If you need an orthopedic surgeon, if you go to his office it takes you a month. But you can do it in a day if you come here.

As noted earlier, there is some concern over the quality of care in the ER, and attempts are now under way to introduce mechanisms that are likely to affect quality positively. How successful such a program will be is no doubt directly related to the ability of some group members to influence others. It is obvious that this development is working in a neutral environment, where those responsible for monitoring the care are most worried about their own practices, and those delivering the care are most concerned with the day's immediate crises. The hospital, the third force, has seemingly taken a hands-off approach to this so-called professional area.

Other forces that are likely to affect developments at Mercy Hospital are the new affiliations with the State Medical College and the commission that has been set up in the state to monitor and regulate hospital costs. The affiliation is described as:

> an affiliation in which they are thinking of sending some of their students in certain areas. They're interested, they said, in the ambulatory care, primary care area. But I think that they sort of envision this as an O.E.O. kind of primary care. And they had envisioned that this is a kind of continuing care that we gave. We don't. I don't know—I haven't talked with them further about this particular area. They're interested in medicine and fellowships in medicine; they're also interested in sending their house staff up here, possibly in mental health... and when the internship and residency requirements change in 1975, I don't know whether we'll be able to get the appropriate number of residents or not. Probably there'll be some shifting around, in which case we'll affiliate with some school so that we can get these internships of which parts of our services are used.

Perhaps the medical school will influence the hospital into becoming something other than what some have described as a "doctors' workshop." Such developments are not without precedent and often involve staff bloodshed.

The second force—the State Health Care Cost Commission—requires that hospitals submit their annual budgets and capital expenditures for review and approval. It is not inconceivable that, like the federal government under Phase IV, the Commission will attempt to influence the hospital in the direction of cutting inpatient days in lieu of more ambulatory services.

THE FUTURE

Evolutionary change in the administrative structure of ambulatory care is foreseen, but not for several years. Despite the obvious problem of coordination and duplication, pressure for change is limited because of the general financial solvency of the various ambulatory care areas; the significant constituencies of each of the department heads; and the fact that the community, which is vocal and powerful, is generally satisfied, while the disenfranchised in the community have not rallied around health care as a major problem.

Thus, despite the lack of primary care physicians in neighboring communities and the inability of some people to have access to affordable care, there seems to be little pressure on the hospital to take the initiative to change. For example, the town contributes approximately $100,000 per year to the hospital, and its local councilman occasionally extracts some political mileage by complaining about symptomatic problems, but no one appears to be pushing the hospital into a more assertive posture with respect to fulfilling community health needs.

COMMENT

In many regards, the Mercy Hospital is a success story. The active physicians at the hospital are eminently qualified practitioners. The hospital is well-equipped; indeed, some departments, such as nuclear medicine and the laboratory, are as good as or better than those found in medical center teaching hospitals. Finally, the ER group is no doubt a vast improvement over nurses screening patients and calling for an on-duty physician regardless of specialty. So what is the problem? For the individual patient and the public, the problems are subtle. For example, the hospital has developed what appears to be a service that fills the primary care vacuum in the area. But what is missing is a commitment to provide or coordinate a wide range of services to a defined population, whether that population is a community or simply multiple and continuous users of the emergency room.

The public is paying for a hospital-based group practice that specializes in episodic primary care. Two problems must be faced. First, is such a system a cost-effective way of handling the type of primary care that crowds emergency rooms? Second, is a Mercy-type organization a step forward or backward in a hospital's assuming responsibility for the "doctorless" patients?

Finally, for the hospital, the problem is uncertainty. Like many institutions, it has been growing at a rapid pace. In the last five years, for example, the budget has more than doubled, ER visits and staffing have doubled, and the environment in which the hospital operates has changed dramatically—witness Phase I through Phase IV and the cost commission. A hospital and its components, such as the ER group, must adapt to these changes while simultaneously planning long-range strategies to meet community needs. How such plans and strategies are being formulated is unclear. How effectively the institution will recognize and respond to the needs of the community remains to be seen.

Chapter 13

Conclusion

A FINAL WORD

First, two true stories:

1. Several years ago, when I was working on the study for the book *Community Hospitals and the Challenge of Primary Care*, I was doing some fieldwork in Rochester, New York. Rochester has a long and distinguished health care track record. Its hospital council, health council, health planning agency, Blue Cross plan, and medical school are among the nation's most progressive and distinguished. Further, and somewhat interestingly, there also appears to be a fair amount of health care competition in that city and, to an outsider such as myself, a higher-than-average level of consciousness about health care in Rochester. One fascinating thing was that there were three competing HMOs in Rochester.

One Monday morning, I arrived at Monroe County Airport, got into a cab and was heading toward Strong Memorial Hospital, when the following exchange took place between me and the cab driver, a Mr. Jake Levine:

Me: Do you know anything about the health plans here in Rochester?
Levine: Yes, a great deal.
Me: How's that?
Levine: Look, I know enough to be sorry I'm not a member. I'm 62. I've had one heart attack and I'm diabetic. I'd certainly profit from being a member of one of those plans.
[I thought to myself, incredible, this guy is really tuned in. OK, now for the $64 question]—
Me: Tell me, Mr. Levine, if you were to join one plan, which would it be?

121

Levine: I don't know—but probably Jack LaLane's Health Spa.

2. When a colleague of mine, Dr. Steve Rosenberg was Commissioner of Public Health in San Bernardino County, California, he visited one of the small towns under his jurisdiction. Some of the community leaders and health practitioners told him they desperately needed his help to get a grant so the town could get a second ambulance. It turned out that the town had one ambulance and needed two. In the past one was sufficient because a local Marine Corps base provided backup. However, the base had been cut back and the second ambulance was no longer available.

Dr. Rosenberg looked at the gross data on ambulance usage and agreed that there was a need for a second vehicle. However, he decided to look beyond the aggregate data, and he found two major clusters of demand. One came from the area where the Mojave Indians lived, and most of those calls were related to the problem of diabetes, such as insulin shock and acidosis (the Mojave Indians have a considerable prevalence of diabetes). The second cluster of calls were coming from a two-lane highway that was a backroad between Los Angeles and Las Vegas. This road had a tremendously high incidence of accidents in the area around the town. Dr. Rosenberg's solution was the institution of the first health education program for the Indians and two stop lights as the highway approached town. The second ambulance was no longer needed.

Better organization and delivery of ambulatory care has been posited as a solution whose time has come. Ambulatory care, it is argued, will substitute for more expensive inpatient care and result in a more rational and more cost-effective health system. What it will also do, it is suggested, is enfranchise doctors and hospitals as monoliths. The already limited ability of patients to do any type of comparison shopping will be further eroded.

The costs and benefits of ambulatory care programs to the providers seem clear—but what about consumers? Are "convenience" and "rationality" an appropriate price? Perhaps so, in a system that has already done so much to preclude free choice.

The organizations considered in this text all had several common elements: they were all intensely concerned about the delivery of primary care services; they had many conflicting objectives; and they were all multi-million-dollar operations with a potential, and sometimes reality, of severely impacting on a local community. Each, though, has an individual personality; and, as is the pattern throughout the health industry, each of these organizations is a conglomeration of complex problems, competing individuals, and disparate programs.

Finally, a noncynical concluding remark—it is amazing and highly creditable that such organizations can respond in somewhat reasonable manner to the health challenge presented to them.

Bibliography

Adam, F.B. "Cooperate with the ER or Compete with It?" *Medical Economics*, November 22, 1971, pp. 174-183.

American Hospital Association. "Reshaping Ambulatory Care Programs," Report and recommendations of a conference on ambulatory care. November 14-17, 1971.

American Medical Association. "Community Health Delivery Programs: Task Force Report." Council on Medical Service, Committee on Community Health Care, 1973.

American Medical Association. *Guidelines for Community Health Programs*. Council on Medical Service, Committee on Community Health Care, 1972.

Beale, E.C. and Schroeder, S.A. *Marketing for an Urban Health Center*, *Health Services Reports* 88, no. 1 (January 1973): 84-88.

Boyd, D.R. "Illinois Emergency Medical Service System Status Report II (July, 1973)." *Illinois Medical Journal*, September 1973, pp. 210-217.

Broske, S.P. and Lerner, M. "Pediatric Residents' Opinions on Solo and Group Practice." *Journal of Medical Education*, November 1971, pp. 971-976.

Busek, L.C. "Why Make Emergency Patients Go to the ER?" *Medical Economics*, March 4, 1974, p. 109.

Bush, A.S. *Group Practice: Planning and Implementing a Community-wide Prepayment Plan for Health Services*. New York State Health Planning Commission, September, 1971.

Carlova, J. "The Economic Case Against Big Groups." *Medical Economics*, November 6, 1972, pp. 178-192.

Claremont, H.E. "Ambulatory Care in a Teaching Hospital: the Group Practice Model." *The Hospital Staff*, January 1974, pp. 16-23.

Conroy, W.J. "What Middle-size Groups Are Made Of." *Group Practice*, December 1973, pp. 7-9.

Courtney, J.F. "Advice to Moonlighters: How to Collect Those ER Fees." *Resident and Staff Physician*, March 1973, pp. 65-73.

Cowen, D.L. "Denver: Neighborhood Health Centers, Operating Within an Integrated System, Provide Dignified, Comprehensive Care for All." *Hospitals*, July 1, 1970, pp. 61-64.

Crichton, A.O.J. and Anderson, D.O. *Group Practice in the System: An Enquiry in Efficient and Effective Organization of Medical Practice.* Vol. II of *A Study of Economies of Group Practice in Saskatchewan.* Office of the Co-ordinator, Health Sciences Centre, University of British Columbia, 1973.

Davis, M.M. "Reminiscences and Prospectives in Ambulatory Services." *Bulletin N.Y. Acad. Med.*, January 1965, pp. 132-138.

DeHoff, J.B. "Emergency Departments: Multi-Purpose Medical Centers." *Maryland State Medical Journal*, February 1972, pp. 55-76.

Ellwood, P.M. "Health Maintenance Organizations: Concept and Strategy." *Hospitals*, March 1971, pp. 53-56.

Falk, L.A. "Functional Group Practice in a National Health Program." *Yale Journal of Biology and Medicine*, August, 1971, pp. 153-159.

Falick, J. "Instant Architecture for Ambulatory Care: Build Fast but Build to Last." *Modern Hospital*, March 1975, pp. 59-62.

Freeark, R.J. "The Surgeon's Role in the Staffing of Hospital Departments." *The Journal of Trauma*, April 1973, pp. 300-306.

Freidson, E., and Mann, J.H. "Organizational Dimensions of Large-scale Group Practice." *A.J.P.H.*, April 1971, pp. 786-795.

Freilich, H. "A Guide to Improved Ambulatory Care Service." *Hospital Management*, March 1969, pp. 52-55.

Gibson, G. "EMS: A Facet of Ambulatory Care." *Hospitals*, May 16, 1973, pp. 59-66.

Gibson, G. "Guidelines for Research and Evaluation of Emergency Medical Services." *Health Services Reports*, March-April 1974, pp. 99-111.

Glasgow, J.M. "Prepaid Group Practice as a National Health Policy: Problems and Perspectives." *Inquiry*, March 1972, pp. 3-15.

Hannas, R.R. "Emergency Department Physician Staffing Patterns and Residency Training." *Illinois Medical Journal*, June 1973, pp. 525-526.

Hannas, R.R. "Staffing the Emergency Depart." *Hospitals*, May 16, 1973, pp. 83-86.

Hardy, C.T. "Are You the Group Practice Type?" *Medical Economics*, October 31, 1968, pp. 100-104.

_____. "Don't Let Health Planners Plan Without You." *Medical Economics*, May 25, 1970, p. 252.

_____. "Group Practice by Medical School Faculty." *Journal of Medical Education*, August 1968, pp. 907-911.

_____. "Help Patients Collect Medicare Claims?" *Medical Economics*, April 3, 1967, pp. 141-153.

_____. "How Are Your Business Ethics?" *Medical Economics*, September 3, 1968, pp. 68-71.

_____. "How Do You Handle Hospital Mix-ups?" *Medical Economics*, January 8, 1968, pp. 147-158.

_____. "How to Outwit a Hospital Administrator." *Medical Economics*, December 11, 1967, pp. 80-83.

_____. "Inside Tips to Smooth Referrals to a Medical Center." *Medical Economics*, March 2, 1970, pp. 77-80.

_____. "Institution-related Group Practice: Best of Both Worlds?" *Hospital Physician*, February 1969, pp. 75-122.

_____. "Institutionally-Based Groups." *Group Practice*, September 1968, pp. 36-39.

_____. "Is the Wrong Person Listening?" *Hospital Physician*, October, 1965, pp. 195-202.

_____. "What'll Make M.D.'s Go Where They're Needed?" *Medical Economics*, June 10, 1968, pp. 63-67.

_____. "When Patients Clash with Hospital Personnel." *Hospital Physician*, September 1968, pp. 85-94.

Harper, B.C. "Continuity of Care." *Hospitals, JAHA*, April 1, 1973, pp. 115-118.

Heyssel, R.M. "HMOs: Prototypes: Maryland: The Columbia Medical Plan and the East Baltimore Medical Plan." *Hospitals*, March 16, 1971, pp. 69-71.

Hill, D.B. and Veney, J.D. "Kansas Blue Cross/Blue Shield Outpatient Benefits Experiment." *Medical Care*, March-April, 1970, pp. 143-158.

Holliday, J.E. "East is East and West is West (and Groups are Different All Over)." *Group Practice*, September 1972, pp. 30-32.

Jackson, T.L. "Emergency Medical Care in the Inner-City." *Urban Health*, August 1974, pp. 43 & 70.

Jacobs, A.R. "Emergency Department Utilization in an Urban Community: Implications for Community Ambulatory Care." *JAMA*, April 12, 1971, pp. 307-312.

Johnson, W.L. and Rosenfeld, L.S. "Factors Affecting Waiting Time in Ambulatory Care Services." *Health Services Research*, Winter 1968, pp. 286-295.

Kaiser, E.F. "One Industry's Involvement in Health Care." *Journal Of Medical Education*, February 1970, pp. 88-95.

Katz, G. "Pilot Study of Medical Practices in Medical Arts Buildings." *Public Health Reports*, November 1966, pp. 1025-1030.

Kerr, G.M. "A New Concept in Ambulatory Care: The Planning and Design of the New Ambulatory Unit at New Mount Sinai Hospital, Toronto." *Canadian Hospital*, April 1972, pp. 54-61.

Kovner, J.W., Brown, L.B., and Kisch, A. I. "Income and the Use of Outpatient Medical Care by the Insured." *Inquiry* VI, no. 2: 27-34.

Kralewski, J.E. and Bauer, J.C. "The HMO as a Resource Allocator." *The Hospital Medical Staff*, April 1974, pp. 3-8.

Krembs, G.A. "Contracting with a Physicians' Group for ER Coverage." *Hospital Progress*, January 1970, pp. 51-53.

Lee, R.K.C. "Preventive Medicine in a Private Group Practice Setting." *Arch. Environ. Health*, September 1971, pp. 226-229.

Leveson, I. "The Demand for Neighborhood Medical Care." *Inquiry* VII, no. 4: 17-24.

Mahoney, A.R. "Factors Affecting Physicians' Choice of Group or Independent Practice." *Inquiry*, June 1973, pp. 9-18.

Mamlin, J.J. and Baker, D.H. "Combined Time-Motion and Work Sampling Study in a General Medicine Clinic." *Medical Care*, September-October 1973, pp. 449-456.

McCormack, R.C. and Miller, C. "The Economic Feasibility of Rural Group Practice: Influence of Non-physician Practitioners." *Primary Care*, January-February 1972, pp. 73-80.

McNamara, E. and Todd, C. "A Survey of Group Practice in the United States, 1969." *AJPH*, July 1970, pp. 1,303-1,313.

Monoghan, J.C. "Solving a Family Doctor Shortage: The ER Switch." *Medical Economics*, January 21, 1974, pp. 193-198.

Neely, J.R. "Health Maintenance Organizations: Guidelines for Implementation." *Hospitals*, pp. 79-81.

Neumann, H.H. "Capitation Prepayment: Without Formal Group Practice." *Medical Care*, March-April, 1970, pp. 159-160.

O'Donnell, E. "Ambulatory Patients Don't Belong in Hospitals." *Medical Economics*, December 9, 1974, pp. 157-169.

Owens, A. "Why Aren't Primary-Care Doctors More Productive?" *Medical Economics*, April 1, 1974, pp. 89-93.

Paxton, H.T. "They Moonlight in Their Own ER." *Hospital Physician*, February 1970, p. 137.

Prussin, J.A. "HMOs: Organizational And Financial Models." *Hospital Progress*, April 1974, pp. 33-35.

Reinhardt, U.E. "Manpower Substitution and Productivity in Medical Practice: Review of Research." *Health Services Research*, Fall, 1973, pp. 200-227.

Reuter, L.F. "Providing Room to Care." *Hospitals, JAHA*, February 16, 1974, pp. 62-65.

Richmond, G.M. *Ambulatory Care: An Annotated Bibliography of Recent Planning Research.* Syracuse, New York, Areawide and Local Planning for Health Action, Inc., 1973.

Roemer, Milton I. "Group Practice: A Medical-Care Spectrum." *Journal of Medical Education*, December 1965, pp. 1154-1158.

Shockett, E. "Group vs. Solo Practice, Letter to Editor." *JAMA*, February 21, 1972, p. 1067.

Snedecor, S.T. "The Director of the Emergency Department, Editorial." *The Journal of Trauma*, December 1971, pp. 1054-1056.

Taubenhaus, L.J. "The Nonscheduled Patient in the Emergency Department and Walk-in Clinic." *Bulletin N.Y. Acad. Med.* 49, no. 5 (May 1973): 419-426.

———. "Emergency Services." *Hospitals*, April 1, 1972, pp. 81-85.

U.S. Dept. of Health, Education, and Welfare, Social Security Administration Office of Research and Statistics, Health Insurance Statistics. *Impact of Cost-Sharing on Use of Ambulatory Services Under Medicare: Preliminary Findings, 1969.* DHEW Pub. No. (SSA) 74-11702, October 1973.

Vorzimer, J.J. and Winter, R. "Team approach Yields Comprehensive Care." *Hospitals*, August 16, 1972, pp. 61-66.

Webb, S.B. and Fenhagen, H.P. "Full-time Emergency Department Physicians." *The Hospital Medical Staff*, July 1973, pp. 10-17.

Webb, S.B. and Lawrence, R.W. "Physician Staffing and Reimbursement Trends." *Hospitals*, October 1, 1972, pp. 69-75.

White, R.R. "A Surgeon Looks at Group Practice." *Archives of Surg.*, April 1972, pp. 393-396.

Wooldridge, W.E. "How Good Are the Superclinics?" *Medical Economics*, April 26, 1971, pp. 103-151.

Index

About the Author

Seth B. Goldsmith is now on the faculty of the School of Public Health at the University of Massachusetts at Amherst. From 1972 to 1977, Dr. Goldsmith was on the faculty of the Columbia University School of Public Health, where he was director of the Graduate Program in Health Services Administration and an assistant professor. Educated at New York University (B.S., 1961), Columbia University (M.S., 1963), and The Johns Hopkins University (Sc.D., 1970), Dr. Goldsmith has also served on the faculties of the University of the Philippines, George Washington University, The Naval School of Hospital Administration, and Tulane University. He has acted as consultant to various hospitals and organizations such as the World Health Organization, the New York City Health Serivces Administration, the National Planning Association, and the Robert Wood Johnson Foundation. He is the author of *Prison Health* (Prodist, 1975), co-author of *Community Hospitals and Primary Care* (Ballinger, 1976), and numerous articles on various aspects of health administration.